Follow

The

Solid

Rock

Road

Pathway to Radical Recovery

Jamee Rae Pineda
& Sherry Colby
www.thesolidrockroad.com

ZIKLAG International
P.O. Box 1057, Phoenix, OR 97535

FIRST EDITION

By Ziklag International

Scriptures are taken from the New King James Version, unless otherwise noted.

ISBN 978-0-615-33789-0

ISBN 061-533-7899

The Solid Rock Road logo design by Natalie Schmelzer

In honor of our mother and father

Jim Harkness, our dad
A man who viewed life in black and white and wasn't afraid to say so. Thanks dad, for your safe lap, your firm hand, and words of encouragement. Thanks for loving mom and demonstrating the heart of a father.

Diane (Dugie) Harkness, our mom
The most honest woman we know. Thanks mom, for providing a wonderful home life and for teaching us what it means to love your husband and children. Sorry for making you worry so much...and for so long.

Special thanks to:

Karen Fronek of Make It Happen for your never-ending support and coaching.

Pete Miller, Amy Miller, and Craig Fronek for your proofreading and editing skills.

Bill and Nancie Carmichael for early manuscript critiques.

HOW TO USE THIS BOOK

Follow The Solid Rock Road takes you on an experiential journey of discovery. Each of the 10 Principles challenges you to incorporate higher-level habits into your Christian life.

We aren't shaking a finger at you and telling you how bad you've been—even though you may have been very bad. Instead, we're guiding you through some important spiritual concepts so you can fully understand the battle you face and what the Bible says to do. The goal is to make sure you don't spend a lifetime coping with your addiction, but that you are set free from your addiction once and for all.

You can read this book all the way through, then read it again and do the exercises, or do the work as you go. Either way, we have made reading easier by creating icons and conventions, as follows:

When you see this icon, it means Sherry is speaking. When she's done, you'll see a ■.

When you see this icon, it means Jamee is speaking. When she's done, you'll see a ■.

 Exercise When you see this shaded Exercise box, you will spend time thinking things through and writing down your answers. We suggest you get a special journal to use with this book. That way, you'll have a record of what God showed you, and the steps you should take to transform you life.

▶ When you see this arrow, you'll read pull quotes, which help to highlight important information.

FOREWARD

By Pastor Steve Schmelzer

Wow! Isn't this book timely! As a seminal approach in a world needing drug and alcohol solutions, this could just be that book.

Jamee Rae Pineda and Sherry Colby have written a groundbreaking book with *Follow The Solid Rock Road: Pathway to Radical Recovery,* which addresses a deep philosophical split in drug and alcohol treatment.

While most addiction treatments keep people on a perpetual path of coping, Jamee and Sherry open the door to freedom in God and set people on the path to achieve it. Initially, this path doesn't seem to differ much from existing recovery systems, but it ultimately results in irreconcilable differences.

Follow The Solid Rock Road teaches that one finds freedom through the teachings of Jesus Christ, His atonement, and having an honest walk with God. The 10 Principles of The Solid Rock Road describe how one can identify their addiction, address their addiction, and subsequently be delivered from it.

This work is not bogged down with stodgy or clinical verbiage but is interspersed with anecdotal evidence that illustrates how these principles work. The personal stories from the lives of Jamee and Sherry are transparent and refreshing. Thank you for this level of honesty. It is quite helpful in showing that the 10 Bible-based Principles are more than untested theories, but instead have been applied and proven.

The book is sprinkled with life application exercises and hard-hitting questions. When completed, these will bring a person to self awareness and true change. This is a valuable handbook for life transformation.

Another important aspect of this book is that it can be used individually or in group settings. The final great feature is that the authors offer personal help and interaction for those involved in this process – the addicted, loved ones of the addicted, ministry leaders, and pastors.

As stated in this book, why walk The Yellow Brick Road when we can get on The Solid Rock Road?

TABLE OF CONTENTS

Introduction: Get Off the Yellow Brick Road   1

Principle 1: Surrender and Realize Your Need for God   7

Principle 2: Empty Yourself of Your Sinful Nature   25

Principle 3: Pray and Meditate on the Word of God   47

Principle 4: Forgive Yourself and Others   85

Principle 5: Be Accountable and Be Vulnerable   113

Principle 6: Stay Close to God – Praise & Worship   139

Principle 7: Seek the Will of God for Your Life   153

Principle 8: Stay on the Path God Leads You To   163

Principle 9: Be Ready for Battle – Full Armor of God   193

Principle 10: Serve God and Others   215

Afterward: The Next Best Steps   237

Introduction: Get Off the Yellow Brick Road

"This is what the LORD says: "Stand at the Crossroads and look; ask for the ancient paths, ask where the good way is, and walk in it, and you will find rest for your souls."
—Jeremiah 6:16

Our whole family watched the Wizard of Oz the day we got our first color TV. We were young girls at the time and could hardly wait to see the movie. We were instantly infatuated with Dorothy and hated the mean and ugly lady on the bicycle. As the movie progressed, we went from being awestruck with all the color and characters to scared senseless.

In the movie, Dorothy gets tossed around in a tornado and wakes up in Munchkinland. Her house lands on top of the Wicked Witch of the East and kills her. Thankfully, Glinda the Good Witch of the North appears to ease Dorothy's mind and give her the magical ruby red slippers from the feet of the dead witch. Soon after, the Wicked Witch of the West shows up to terrify Dorothy – and the two of us!

The Wicked Witch of the West is angry that Dorothy is wearing the ruby red slippers. She makes it clear that her plan is to take them from her.

With threats from the Wicked Witch looming, Glinda and the well-meaning Munchkins direct Dorothy to the Yellow Brick Road. They assure the girl in the blue checkered dress that the road will lead her to Emerald City and the great Wizard of Oz who has the power to get her home. So off Dorothy and her little dog Toto go, completely oblivious to the danger and disappointment that lay ahead.

Along the way, Dorothy befriends the scarecrow, tin man, and cowardly lion, all searching for something to make them more complete. Together, they follow the Yellow Brick Road, believing that the Wizard will perform multiple miracles on their behalf.

Though pursued by the Wicked Witch of the West, Dorothy and her three companions finally find refuge behind the huge doors of Oz. Then, by accident, they discover that the Wizard is all smoke and mirrors – powerless to give the scarecrow a brain, the tin man a heart, or the cowardly lion courage. Worse yet, the phony Wizard is without power to return Dorothy to Kansas.

Like a good witch should, Glinda re-appears just in time. Glinda tells Dorothy that she already has the power to return home – if she simply clicks the heels of her ruby red slippers and repeats the phrase, "There's no place like home." Dorothy follows the beautiful witch's instructions and is immediately whisked back to Kansas and her beloved family.

While the Wizard of Oz is a much-loved movie classic, we've never understood why the Good Witch waited to tell Dorothy about the power of the ruby red slippers. We wondered why Glinda sent the lost young woman down the Yellow Brick Road when there was a faster, easier, and safer way home.

The Real Yellow Brick Road

Today, millions of Christians are directed to a modern-day Yellow Brick Road to recovery from addictions. They are assured by the treatment industry that sobriety is found along many paths and in *a* higher power, not *the* higher power.

People battling addictions get to choose from an array of recovery methods, modalities, therapies, spiritual philosophies, and programs on their journey along the Yellow Brick Road. They're also given a long list of excuses for their inability to get and stay sober. We've used a few ourselves.

Anxiety, depression, ADHD, Post Traumatic Stress Disorder (PTSD), low self-esteem, and abusive parents are a few reasons addicts give to justify actions. The pre-treatment cure is often a stabilizing pill, which offers a temporary and false sense of well-being. (As ex-addicts, we find it hard to believe that drugs are used to treat addictive personalities. It's one of the many ironies of life.)

Before anyone gets offended, we acknowledge that mental health issues exist and realize that people have suffered, been mistreated, molested, neglected, and rejected. We've had our share of pain, so we have true compassion for anyone who has endured hardship and difficult circumstances.

Still, there comes a time when your past should no longer determine your future – when you leave your old life for a brand new one and enact the new creation reality that God made available through His Son, Jesus Christ.

It's good to reflect on your life. There's value in acknowledging the mistakes you've made and learning from the pain others have caused you. But Philippians 3:13 tells us to look ahead, *"...forgetting those things which are behind and reaching forward to those things which are ahead."*

The Solid Rock Road

By reading this book, we pray you would fully understand the spiritual battle in the unseen world, the purpose of Christ's suffering on the cross, and the transforming power of God.

While Dorothy faced danger and distress along the Yellow Brick Road, she finally turned to her ruby red slippers. With a few clicks of her heels and a little bit of faith, Dorothy's problems were quickly solved. She returned home to Auntie Em. She got her life back.

> **Like the ruby red slippers for Dorothy, the red blood of Jesus Christ gives you all the power you need to turn things around.**

When you choose to follow The Solid Rock Road, you find your way home. From the Old Testament to the New, the solid rock represents the foundation and teachings of Jesus Christ. From them, you can build an amazing, addiction-free life. You can wake up with hope, and live a productive and respectable life. You will also discover your destiny and leave a legacy for generations to come.

Like the ruby red slippers for Dorothy, the red blood of Jesus Christ gives you all the power you need to turn things around. It can immediately cleanse, heal, and restore your life. You don't have to travel far or wait a long time for the blood to work. It has been poured out for you in advance and in abundance. The blood of Jesus is readily available on your journey to radical recovery.

The Wicked Witch of the West wanted to steal Dorothy's slippers because she knew of their magical powers. The same is true for the devil who wants to steal your Christian power from you. If you continue in your addictions or take an unnecessary jaunt along the Yellow Brick Road to recovery, you won't find a witch or evil flying monkeys, but you may find yourself being constantly pursued by the devil and his evil spirits.

What You'll Learn

In this book, you'll learn a lot about yourself, God, the Holy Spirit, and Jesus Christ. You'll also become very familiar with the enemy of mankind and how to fight and win the battle for your own soul. We're taking you on an experiential journey that gets you home in a hurry, and gives you all the Biblical tools needed to protect yourself, along with everyone else who is in your sphere of influence.

You don't need magic to make your life great. You need the blood of Jesus and to learn the wonderful ways of God. You need to follow The Solid Rock Road, which is your pathway to radical recovery.

Our Disclaimer

We're not against secular treatment programs. We know they're necessary and the world needs trained counselors who care. However, we've written this book from a Christian perspective. We're reaching Christians who continually struggle with addictions, as well as Christians in recovery who are ready to move forward in their lives and ministries.

We are also writing for pastors, Christian leaders, and those heading up recovery ministries who are ready for a purely Bible-based system that promotes the new creation reality and assimilation into the Body of Christ.

If you're not a Christian but looking for spiritual answers to resolve your addictions issues, you'll find them here. Plus, you'll get to learn what Christians believe and why we choose a spiritually progressive lifestyle that brings change and results in purposeful living.

God is Enough!

This book reminds the Christian community that God is enough. The Word of God must take precedence in a Christian's life – over the education, science, systems, counsel, and philosophies of any and all secular treatment programs and organizations.

In other words, do what God has instructed you to do. Follow The Solid Rock Road and steer clear of every other path. That's how you'll win the battle for your own soul and model a purpose-filled Christian life for your children and generations to come.

Principle 1: Surrender and Realize Your Need for God

"My grace is sufficient for you, for my power is made perfect in weakness. Therefore I will boast all the more gladly about my weaknesses, so that Christ's power may rest on me." (NIV)
— 2 Corinthians 12:9

Do you believe that God is enough?

Don't be too quick to answer "yes." If you agree, then you're without excuse for your addictions. If God is enough, His power gives you strength to quit once and for all. Not only that, God's presence offers peace of mind in the process of change, and His Word provides all the wisdom and inspiration you need to keep moving forward in a positive direction.

If you know in your heart that God is enough, but continue in your addictions, you are disobedient, rebellious, and self-willed. There's no getting around it, and no easier way to say it. You have what you need to get your life back, but you still refuse to do what's necessary to reclaim it.

Fortunately, God understands matters of the heart and gives us a certain amount of leeway as we walk out our Christianity. But God has limits. Yes, He gives grace, but there are two kinds of grace. One is saving grace, and the other is the enabling power of God that ensures you can resist all temptation.

At some point, God expects you to quit resisting Him and instead follow His commands.

Phrases used to describe the word 'command' in Merriam-Webster's dictionary include "to direct authoritatively" as well as to "exercise a dominating influence." This may explain your problem. You don't want to submit to authority and you don't want anyone to dominate your life.

If you acknowledge that's true, you would be wise to repent. If you don't repent of your disobedience, or you have false remorse, you will continue in your addictions because you're more aligned with the ways of the world than the ways of God.

Romans 12:2 helps makes this point: *"And do not be conformed to this world, but be transformed by the renewing of your mind, that you may prove what is that good and acceptable and perfect will of God."*

Doubting is Sin

Perhaps the first step in your journey to radical recovery is to admit you haven't believed that God is enough. There's no shame in making such a confession if that really is your truth. However, once you've acknowledged a lack of faith or limited understanding of who God is, you are responsible for doing something about it.

No one can force truth down your throat, nor is God going to place a spiritual feeding tube in you. You have to want it and you have to get it yourself. There's plenty of spiritual food to go around. At church, your pastor is at the pulpit preaching his guts out. Your Bible is full of the inspired Word of God. If you have doubt, then you would be wise to become obsessed with scriptures about faith, the heroes of faith, and hang around people who consistently demonstrate faith.

Whether you lack faith, don't fully understand Christian principles, or are just being stubborn, your only hope in overcoming your addictions and living a blessed life is to completely surrender to God.

What my client needed was supernatural heart surgery and a divine brain transplant. She needed the mind of Christ and the heart of God – the purest form of recovery.

You can resist all you want or whine about how your situation is harder or worse than everyone else's, but God can't be manipulated by your tears, fears, or false promises. And if you believe that your addiction is stronger than His power to set you free, then your message to the world is that Christ's suffering on the cross was meaningless to you.

🔊 Divine Healing

Years ago when working in a treatment center as a level two certified drug and alcohol counselor (CADCII), I was waiting to meet with a client who had relapsed. I prayed and asked God to help me give the right advice to this woman whom I'd come to love. I pictured many gaping wounds with tiny bandages that were failing to stop her bleeding. I realized that nothing I learned in college, and nothing we offered at the center, would help her stay clean forever. I knew God was her real answer, but He wasn't allowed in our sessions.

All the education courses, parenting classes, group sessions, and every program my client participated in were like temporary patches, not cures. She needed supernatural heart surgery and a divine brain transplant, which is the mind of Christ and the heart of God – the purest form of recovery. ∎

God Wants It All

It's true that God performs miracles. We've seen them happen and have experienced more than our fair share. But if God isn't giving you a miracle related to your addiction, it's possible He doesn't want to be your situational rescuer.

God won't put a bandage on your gaping wound, although He has held you together while waiting to perform surgery on you. He hasn't scheduled the surgery so far because God first wants you to cling to your salvation and make Jesus the Lord of your life. He wants you to realize you need Him all the time and more than you need anything else in the world. God doesn't want half of your heart or part of your mind. He wants it all. That's because He wants you to be complete in Him.

When you fully surrender, we guarantee you'll find the strength and courage you need to quit addictive behaviors. You won't have to go into a treatment center or offer a lifelong commitment to a recovery organization. You won't have to claim that you are an addict until the day you die. In fact, you should visualize yourself free from your addiction now and claim you are done with it forever.

Admit you're weak and you need God's intervention. Let go of all that you hold onto, and release your life into the hands of the Most High. Then walk boldly down The Solid Rock Road to recovery and stay on it.

Looking for the Answer

We're guessing you have tried to quit drinking or drugging more times than you can count. Your own willpower, the wisdom of counselors, instructions from probation officers, pleadings from loved ones, testimonies of peers, and horrific personal consequences may have pushed you to quit for a time, but didn't keep you straight for good. You have wondered if anything will.

You're not alone. We've counseled hundreds of people just like you, searching high and low for a way out of their addictions. Before surrendering to God, we were there, waking up every morning with a promise to quit. But neither of us could resist the temptation because we did not understand the power of surrendering to God.

As those who know how you think, we believe some of you are considering closing this book right now and sticking it on your shelf with all the other self-help or inspirational books that didn't offer you an easy way out. Don't give in.

**Don't do this for your mother, your boss, or your spouse who has threatened to leave you.
Do this for you and for God.**

Everything worthwhile requires effort. Isn't there a lot of work involved with scoring drugs and paying for a good drunk? We won't go into details, but we've come up with many creative financing plans to pay for our partying and have hassled for hours trying to track down a dealer. You surely have many stories of your own to tell, but what we all know is that you considered the end result well worth the effort.

Living a sober and spiritual life is worth all your effort.

Close and Lock the Doors
If you've tried to quit and haven't, you have left a door open to your addiction somewhere along the way. In

this chapter, we'll help you close and lock those doors once and for all through the process of surrender.

Be warned. We won't ask you to surrender halfway, or almost all the way. We're looking for complete surrender because that's what God wants. When you've completely surrendered, you discover that you're complete in Him.

Don't do it for your mother, your boss, or even your spouse who has threatened to leave you. Do it for you and for God. That's the only way it will work. You have to want recovery as much as those who love you, and you have to want God more than you want anything else.

If you're motivated, have a spiritual desire to change from the inside out, and are willing to do whatever it takes, you're committing to radical recovery along The Solid Rock Road. You're saying 'yes' to God and 'no' to the sin of addiction. You're one step closer to living the life that God planned from the beginning. And everything God creates is good.

Making Choices

Every decision has a consequence and lasting effect. One bad decision can change your life forever, and damage many others along the way. How many bad decisions have you made in the last several years? How many arrests and DUIIs are part of your criminal record? Have you missed work or gotten fired after a single night of partying turned into several in a row? Have you mistreated your spouse or your children during a binge?

We've watched a lot of people push their minds, bodies, and souls beyond physical and spiritual boundaries. How far can you push yours?

If you're thinking that your addiction hasn't sunken to the lows of others, you are no better off than someone unwilling to recognize they've hit bottom for the tenth time. If you drink or do drugs more than you should, more than you want, more than you intend, and more than your conscience says is okay, then you are in trouble. You need godly intervention and you must completely surrender yourself to Him.

What is Surrender?

According to Merriam-Webster's dictionary, the definition of surrender is "to yield or relinquish possession or control of one's person into the power of another." Therefore, surrender means you have to quit doing things your way and do it someone else's way. (Interesting how this relates to the word 'command.')

You may think there's freedom in your choice to use drugs or alcohol, and yet you are in complete surrender to your addiction. When you're actively using, you're under the power of the intoxicant and surrendered to the devil's plan for your life.

If you've tried to quit and can't, it's proof you have no control whatsoever. It would be so much better to quit letting Satan rule you through drugs and alcohol. Why not surrender to God whose power is always used for good?

If you're like us, self-will, independence, and rebellion are deeply rooted. We've had years of experience doing our own thing. We want to run the show. Our family, friends, and God tend to get in the way. Thankfully, we made the choice to give God what He wanted, and we're thankful for that decision. Today, we don't let our sin nature overpower our God nature. We do have to fight to keep good thoughts, but that's only possible in a submitted state of mind.

To surrender and submit means you're no longer in control and that you trust God's ways and count on His power. You're admitting that you're weak, which is exactly what God has been waiting for. In 2 Corinthians 12:9, the Apostle Paul writes that the Lord spoke to him during a time of temptation, saying,

"My grace is sufficient for you, for My strength is made perfect in weakness..."

God's grace in Paul's situation, and yours, literally means unmerited favor and undeserved blessing. But it only comes when we wave the white flag in complete surrender to our Creator.

Why is it so hard to give in to God when you are so willing to wave the white flag to temptation, giving in to something you know is destroying your life? It doesn't make sense, but that's because you're under the influence of Satan, and you don't like being told what to do because he doesn't like it.

It's time to think and act differently. When you're under the influence of the Holy Spirit, you'll have a good time along The Solid Rock Road.

Surrender lets you unwind from the world. You don't have to create any more schemes, excuses, or lies to keep your addictions at bay.

Results of Surrender

Relief is the first sign that you have surrendered and realized your need for God. David said it best in Psalm 62:1 *"My soul finds rest in God alone..." (NIV).*

Your addiction has kept you tied in knots, so there is no rest for your weary soul. Surrender lets you unwind from the world. You don't have to create any more schemes, excuses, or lies to keep your addiction issues at bay. Also, there's nothing to fix, so the time you once spent on damage control can be better spent on living a good life.

When surrendered, you quit deciding what you will or won't do. Instead, you do whatever God wants. When you have truly given yourself over to God, you quit making promises you know you can't keep. You feel better all the way around. Things begin to make sense and fall into place naturally. You're thankful and feel happy. You start to notice all the miracles, big and small.

When you're willing to change and grow spiritually, God sends people to support you. You need guidance and you should be accountable to people who have the wisdom and righteousness you need. This can be your pastor, a Christian mentor, or someone who is called into a recovery ministry.

Notice we didn't say someone in recovery. We said someone called into a recovery ministry. There's a big difference and you'll learn about this as you keep reading.

As a surrendered child of God, everything comes together naturally. You are no longer in a constant struggle to survive. You are transformed through a God process. Your heart, mind, and spirit come alive. You feel it and others see it in you.

As your mind gets renewed, and your hard heart softens, all your relationships get better. You stop telling lies or manipulating the people you love. You are transparent and vulnerable, no longer attempting to make up for bad behavior and insane choices. You quit looking for love in all the wrong places.

Many addictive behaviors are rooted in the need to be loved. Let God love you! Realize that you are His beloved child and that He loved you enough to send His Son to die for you. You can't know a greater love than that!

Surrender Your Self-Esteem
We're going against traditional thought when we tell you to surrender your self-esteem. Secular counselors are trained to help you develop and increase it. In fact, low self-esteem is one of the excuses in psychology circles for why people use drugs and alcohol. But as an addict, you have esteemed yourself way too much. Why else would you put your own selfish desires ahead of your friends, family, spouse, and even your children?

If you didn't love yourself too much, how could you spend your rent money on your own pleasures? How could you look into the eyes of your children and easily break so many promises?

We're always blown away by the stories we hear about the sacrifices people make for their drug of choice. In each case, people sacrificed others, not themselves.

> ## Don't use your past as an excuse for your current behavior.

Don't get us wrong. We believe that some people have dealt with traumas that so deflated their soul and spirit they turned to drugs and alcohol for relief. For example, at age eighteen, Sherry was gang raped over an entire weekend by a motorcycle gang called "Unforgiven Sinners." (You'll read all about it in the Forgiveness chapter.) She overheard them plot her murder but was rescued by one of the rapists used by God to spare her life.

Sherry felt unlovable after the rape. As a result, she had a series of abusive relationships and relied on drugs and alcohol to dull the pain of her experiences. The reality is, Sherry suffered real trauma and became addicted and selfish. When she found God, Sherry allowed Him to heal the deep wounds of her experiences. She no longer needed to fill herself with self-affirmations; she studied God's Word and listened carefully to what He said about her.

Quit trying to build yourself up, or look for others to make you feel better about yourself. Don't use your past as an excuse for your current behavior. You may have a real sad story to tell, and we believe you should tell it. But once told, get on with the next phase of your life.

Look around your church and find someone who has given their life to God and whose life is blessed, then do what they do. Then reflect on the people you are now connected with. Are they blessed? Do they inspire you to do well? Would you like your children to grow up to be just like them? If not, then re-evaluate these friendships.

 Start a journal. Even if you don't like to write, make brief notes or bullet points to help you process the information and the experience. These notes will also be useful later. You can return to them when you're struggling in one area or another. Your words serve as a reminder of what God said during this process and what you confirmed as truth.

This is between you and God so answers aren't right or wrong. Be honest, even though you may be used to saying what you think people want to hear. Take this opportunity to get in touch with what you really think, and what's true about your relationship with God.

1. Where does your source of joy come from? Do you have joy, or are you just trying to not be miserable?
2. Who is God to you?
3. What concepts of God were you brought up with and how have they affected your relationship with Him?
4. Do you believe you are worthy of God's love?
5. Do you believe all things are possible with God?
6. What does the word 'surrender' mean to you?
7. What are you willing to give up to follow God wholeheartedly? What won't you give up. Why?
8. Do you believe God is enough?
9. Name one or more incidents in which God expected obedience, but you didn't comply.
10. Are you willing to exchange self-will for God's will?

Prayer of Salvation

We're assuming you believe in God and have faith that His Son Jesus Christ died on the cross as a living sacrifice for your sins. However, if you haven't already given your life to Christ, now is a good time to do so. Christians refer to this as getting saved or being born again.

You can ask Jesus into your heart by repeating the following prayer of salvation:

Dear Heavenly Father:
I realize that I am a sinful person and that I am in need of a savior, so I surrender my life to you. Thank You for sending Your Son Jesus to die for my sake, so I could be forgiven of my sins. I acknowledge that Jesus suffered and died on the cross to take away sins and to stand in my place before God the Father. I also believe that Jesus rose from the dead on the third day.

I'm now asking you to forgive me for the things I've done that have hurt You, my friends, my family, and myself. And, I ask for the gift of eternal life so that when I die, I will go to heaven.

Please help me to turn my life around. I surrender to You. If You'll be my God, I will be Your child. I receive You now, and I ask that You receive me this day. Guide me on Your path, teach me Your ways and help me as I seek Your will for my life. In the name of Jesus, Amen.

Water Baptism

The next step is to get water baptized. We promise it will be the most refreshing dip you've ever taken! You'll go down as the old you and come up as a new person. The Apostle Paul proves this point in 2 Corinthians 5:17: *"Therefore, if anyone is in Christ he is a new creation; old things have passed away; behold, all things have become new."*

If you have already been water baptized, but are making a new commitment to get and stay clean and sober, you may choose to do it again. It's not that your initial baptism is null and void. The new water baptism is symbolic of your coming into the obedience of Christ. It represents your full surrender.

Freedom from Evil Spirits

When you're using drugs and alcohol, you are interacting with the kingdom of darkness. No matter how much self-determination and strength you gather on your own, you don't have enough power to break free from the hold Satan has on you. When you surrender to God, He gives you everything you need, including His power, to fight the battle in the unseen world.

There are two things going on around you every day. One is your life as you experience it. The other is the invisible spirit world where angels, evil spirits, and God exist.

The Bible points out that we are either living in darkness or living in light. Proverbs 4:19 says, *"The way of the wicked is like deep darkness." (NIV)* In John 8:12, Jesus says, *"I am the light of the world. He who follows Me shall not walk in darkness, but have the light of life."*

When you believe that God is enough and you surrender in order to receive His power, you are getting rid of a demonic hold. You are literally exchanging the lies of Satan for the power of God.

There's no doubt that God is more powerful than Satan. Unfortunately, you often see Satan as the one with all the power. You can't resist him because you're surrendered to him. If you transfer your obedience to God, you will be shocked and amazed by His power, love, and grace.

This is your first step to overcoming addictions forever.

God wants to take first place in your life and
be the source of power for all things.

Spiritual Development

This first principle of surrender is accepting that God is enough and Jesus is Lord and Savior. All spiritual development is built on these truths. Your satisfaction will not come from what you do, but in whom you believe. As John 8:32 clearly states: *"And you shall know the truth and the truth shall make you free."*

God wants to take first place in your life and be the source of power for all things. If you have been a Christian for many years but never fully surrendered to God, you are not alone. We have done the same thing. We understood what God wanted, but it wasn't in our hearts to carry out His will. We would cry out to God when we were in pain and in trouble, but ignored Him when life seemed to work.

If we're describing you, don't feel condemned, just make up your mind to change. It's okay to be where you've been, but now is the time to get where you're supposed to go.

The following portion of a poem called "The Choice" was written by Max Lucado from his book, *When God Whispers Your Name.* With permission from the publisher, we're including His words because they are powerful, and they help sum up this chapter.

I Choose Self-Control

I am a spiritual being...
After this body is dead, my spirit will soar.
I refuse to let what will rot, rule the eternal.
I choose self-control.
I will be drunk only by joy.
I will be impassioned only by my faith.
I will be influenced only by God.
I will be taught only by Christ.

I choose self-control.
Love, joy, peace, patience, kindness, goodness,
faithfulness, gentleness, and self-control.
To these I commit my day.
If I succeed, I will give thanks.
If I fail, I will seek His grace.
And then, when this day is done,
I will place my head on my pillow
and rest.

The Surrender Prayer

While understanding the concept of surrender is great, your recovery depends on you *doing* it. So we're ending this chapter by giving you an opportunity to surrender to God right now.

Close your eyes and consider the past, present, and potential consequences of your addiction. Think about all those times you half surrendered along the Yellow Brick Road. Ask yourself, "Have I had enough?"

If you've had enough, picture The Solid Rock Road that leads you straight into the arms of God and keeps you there. Understand that God walks with you along that path, He gives you everything you need to fight the battle, and heaven waits at the end. All along the road are blessings, acceptance, and love, as well as correction, discipline, and direction from a perfect Father.

If you're afraid of the word 'surrender,' think of it like this: Surrender gives you the power of God that gives you the strength you need to get and stay sober forever. Even more, surrender takes your destiny from the hands of the devil, straight into the hands of God. We think surrender is a powerful and positive word. We love it!

Read the following prayer silently first. Then say it out loud with conviction. Picture yourself speaking directly to God who has waited a long time for you to humble yourself and willingly give your life over to Him completely.

Make sure you are either alone or with someone who understands the process you are in. Set the time aside, and don't allow any interruptions.

Dear God:
I'm tired of doing things my way because my way doesn't work. I'm ready to follow The Solid Rock Road because I want right answers and real change. I understand I must completely surrender to Your plans for my life and so I wave my white flag before You. I know You love me and have my best interests at heart. The Bible says You will never leave me nor forsake me. I am Yours, God.

Today is the first day of my journey and I give my destiny to You. I put my life in Your hands with a glad heart, knowing that I'm relying on Your power and strength, not my own. God, I won't hold back anything because

God, You are my counselor, my healer, and my comforter. Thank You for being my Father in heaven. This act of surrender is of my own free will, and by my free will, I put myself under the Lordship of Christ and Your commands. I commit to a lifetime of surrender and ask that You reveal Yourself to me as I open myself to You.

In the name of Jesus, Amen.

Final Words on Surrender

We hope you didn't just read the above prayer, but took it to heart. If you skimmed over it, return to the beginning of the prayer and surrender for real this time!

Don't expect an instant high or some powerful emotion to sweep you off the carpet. That may happen, but you don't need a lightning bolt from heaven to affirm that your prayer worked. God doesn't need to impress you with His power, He is more interested in your faith and obedience. You need to impress Him with your humbled heart.

Now that you have surrendered, tell someone so you are accountable. And when you find yourself trying to control your life, give it back to God. He is much better at managing details than you are.

Keep your surrender prayer nearby. You may want to repeat it because surrender is a process. You need the mind of Christ to let go of control. Without the mind of Christ and the heart of God, you are guided by old thoughts and behaviors. You then begin to reject or question the ways of God. Your desire for drugs and alcohol intensifies, and your resolve to stay clean and sober dissipates.

You'll know you have fully surrendered when you have peace of mind no matter what is going on in your world.

Principle 2: Empty Yourself of Your Sinful Nature

"So I say, live by the Spirit, and you will not gratify the desires of the sinful nature. For the sinful nature desires what is contrary to the Spirit, and the Spirit what is contrary to the sinful nature. They are in conflict with each other, so that you do not do what you want." (NIV)
—Galatians 5:16-17

Evil spirits get very excited when your self-will and disobedience rise up and lead you into temptation. The evil spirits actually expect such behavior because your history proves you have often wavered between good and evil, often choosing to give in to your addictions and other sins instead of standing for God.

Proverbs 26:11 explains the pattern like this: *"As a dog returns to his own vomit, so a fool repeats his folly."*

Vomit is gross and repulsive. It is acidic and filled with poisons that a body has rejected. It's disgusting and it stinks.

In your case, you can compare vomit with drugs and alcohol. Surely you know these substances sour in your system and poison your soul. Since your soul is made up of your mind, will, and emotions, the poison controls the way you think, act, and feel.

When you quit using drugs and alcohol, the poison leaves your system. Your soul is free to love God, and the Holy Spirit is free to do His work. You are on the road to physical, mental, and spiritual recovery.

But the Bible points out that your pattern is to return to your drug of choice or the alcohol that poisoned your soul. When that happens, the Word of God says you are acting like a soul-less, amoral dog, not the Spirit-filled Christian you really are.

Just the thought of the devil's never-ending plan for evil gets our blood boiling!

In order to make lasting changes, you must see the truth and make choices accordingly. If you don't retrain your brain, change your lifestyle, and form higher-level habits, you will always be attracted to your vomit. And you'll always say that God understands your foolishness.

Your sin nature prompts you to do foolish things that go against God and ruin your life. But if you consider the nature of Satan, it makes sense. His purpose on earth is to initiate sin in order to *"kill, to steal, and to destroy"* God's people according to John 10:10. Therefore, it shouldn't come as a surprise that he is absolutely devoted to your relapse.

Just the thought of the devil's never-ending plan for evil gets our blood boiling!

Who is Your Master?
To better understand relapse and its consequences, read 2 Peter 2:19-22: *"...for a man is a slave to*

whatever has mastered him. If they have escaped the corruption of the world by knowing our Lord and Savior Jesus Christ and are again entangled in it and overcome, they are worse off at the end than they were at the beginning. It would have been better for them not to have known the way of righteousness, than to have known it and then to turn their backs on the sacred command that was passed on to them. Of them the proverbs are true: 'A dog returns to its vomit,' and,' A sow that is washed goes back to her wallowing in the mud.'" (NIV)

Had you known it was less dangerous to never be saved than to be saved and relapse, would you have given your life to God? Would you knowingly have claimed Jesus as your Lord and Savior if there was a possibility that you would let Satan return as your master?

We have pondered these questions at length and have concluded that many addicts readily accept salvation, but reject Jesus as Lord. They want to be rescued, but don't want to live by the rescuer's rules, which keep them safe and prevent them from repeating foolish and dangerous behaviors.

People who consistently relapse choose Satan as their master. They want to be free from the constraints of Christian principles so they willingly enter captivity. They like it, then they hate it, then they miss it, then they want it, then they convince themselves they can't quit. This is the perpetual cycle.

In the above scripture (2 Peter 2:19-22), the Apostle Paul writes that even if you wash a pig, it will go back and wallow in the mud. Why? Because it is the nature of a pig to do so. Your nature is to sin and when you agree with Satan to activate your addiction, you wallow in the filth of your decision.

The inspired Word of God compares your sin nature to that of a dog and a pig. And though both dogs and pigs can make good pets, they follow animal instincts.

You, however, are not supposed to act like an animal. You are a spiritual being in a physical body that must connect with God—your source of inspiration and power—in order to operate with Christian instincts. You are made in the image of God.

> **Our original Adam nature lurks about and we often acknowledge and return to it, just like a dog to its vomit and a pig to the mud.**

The Root of Sin

You can trace your propensity for sin back to Adam and Eve who disobeyed God in the Garden of Eden (Genesis 3). Since they were the first people on earth, we are their descendants and inherited their sin nature. That all changed when we were redeemed and reborn into the name of the Lord Jesus Christ.

From that point on, Christ lives in us through the Holy Spirit so we have a new nature that counteracts our natural tendencies — if and when we let it.

No doubt the battle between good and evil rages on. Though we tend to see this battle outside of ourselves, it also takes place on the inside, including our minds, hearts, and souls.

Our original Adam nature lurks about and we often acknowledge and return to it, just like the dog to its vomit and a pig to the mud.

It's easy to blame Adam and Eve for your own propensity to sin. You can also blame Satan and his evil spirits for tempting you. However, you make the choice to let sin control your life when you unleash your Adam nature and give in to drinking, snorting, smoking, or shooting poison into your body.

Lordship

If the blood of Jesus has saved you, then you can't point the finger at evil spirits. If you want to see the real root of your problems, simply look in the mirror and ask if Jesus is your Lord.

To answer truthfully, you should know exactly what the word 'Lord' means. In the Merriam-Webster's dictionary, it is described as "one having power and authority over others, a ruler by hereditary right or preeminence to whom service and obedience are due."

For Jesus to be your Lord, you must serve and obey Him. The Bible takes this a step further. In 1 John 5:3-4 it says that our obedience proves our devotion to God and gives us freedom. *"This is love for God: to obey his commands. And his commands are not burdensome, for everyone born of God has overcome the world." (NIV)*

8 Ongoing Temptations

After I was saved, but before Jesus was my Lord, I sought help from a well-respected psychologist who traced my problems to the trauma of being kidnapped and gang raped at age eighteen. The psychologist diagnosed me with Post Traumatic Stress Disorder and the Stockholm Syndrome.

The psychologist quickly prescribed anti-anxiety and anti-depressant drugs, along with years of therapy to repair the damage done to my psyche. In his final analysis, the psychologist assured me I would feel the effects of the rape for the rest of my life.

My first response after our meeting was to stop at the pharmacy and order my relief in a little bottle. I was glad that someone finally understood my madness and recognized that I had suffered more than the average woman.

As I drove toward Rite Aid to fill the prescriptions, I was suddenly struck by the fact that God was never mentioned in my fifty-seven minutes of therapy. I became so uneasy, I pulled into a parking lot and began to pray. Within seconds, I remembered that God understands me way better than the most prolific psychologist ever could.

God knows my story because He was there. God knows everything I've been through and everything I feel. He sent His son to die so I could be free from my pain and past. Jesus suffered on the cross so I could be set free from my sins and have victory in every area of my life.

I never attended another therapy session with the psychologist or took a single pill for my double disorder. From that point on, I have counted on God's free supernatural therapy to heal my inner wounds and have called on the Holy Spirit to make sure I don't wallow in anxiety and regret. And that's what I do on a daily basis.

Like you, I have to go against my natural way of being and live in the Spirit if I want peace, hope, and happiness every day. I have to quit looking at my experiences and circumstances and stop listening to the lies the devil has been telling me my whole life. I must hear the voice of God.

As Christians, we all have to empty ourselves of our sinful nature so God can fill us with His Holy Spirit. ∎

Changing the Pattern

There is a constant struggle going on inside your mind. It's a war between your old and new self. For people with a history of relapse, the old self often wins. Since the old self is not redeemed, it is still of the world and controlled by Satan. If Satan controls your mind, he becomes the filter by which all information is received. Even the Word of God gets interpreted incorrectly.

Since our minds lead our actions, the devil knows that if we think bad thoughts, we'll act badly. Joyce Meyer wrote a book called *Battlefield of the Mind: Winning the Battle in Your Mind*. In the first chapter, she explains that Satan is strategic and creates deliberates plans to defeat us.

Meyer brings this point home early in her book when she writes, "He (Satan) knows our insecurities, our weaknesses and our fears. He knows what bothers us most. He is willing to invest any amount of time it takes to defeat us. One of the devil's strong points is patience."

With such a patient devil, you must make up your mind to invest any amount of time it takes to defeat him! Even though you surrendered, Satan will wait for the right time to return as your master. He'll wait until you're tired, you're showing signs of weakness, you're having a moment of doubt, or someone at church offended you. He'll wait years if he has to.

So far, you have let Satan win the battle of your mind. But if there is one concept you must believe, it's that when you receive Jesus, you really are a new creation, and that all things really are brand new.

It's time for you to embrace higher-level thinking so you can mature in Christ and live soberly. You can't move forward if you're looking back. You have to keep your eyes on tomorrow and trust that God is who He says He is.

Galatians 4:8-9 explains: *"Formerly, when you did not know God, you were slaves to those who by nature are not gods. But now that you know God—or rather are known by God—how is it that you are turning back to those weak and miserable principles? Do you wish to be enslaved by them all over again?" (NIV)*

If you participate in any of the negative behaviors mentioned in Galatians 5:19-22 (below), then your Adam nature is lurking about. You are losing the battle for your soul, which includes your mind, will, and emotions.

"Now the works of the flesh are evident, which are: adultery, fornication, uncleanness, lewdness, idolatry, sorcery, hatred, contentions, jealousies, outbursts of

wrath, selfish ambitions, dissensions, heresies, envy, murders, drunkenness, revelries, and the like; of which I tell you beforehand, just as I also told you in time past, that those who practice such things will not inherit the kingdom of God." (Gal. 5:19-22)

Empty Yourself

Now that you know your sin nature causes foolish behavior and animal-like conduct, I'm sure you'll agree it's necessary to empty yourself of it. Like surrender, it is a process. Your job is to acknowledge everything that resembles sin in your life, then repent and say goodbye to it.

You will have to empty yourself on a regular basis because certain problem areas tend to pile up. It's like taking out the garbage on trash day. If you remember to pull your can out to the street, the garbage man stops by and empties it. If you forget, your trash piles higher and higher until it eventually overflows. At that point, you have a big mess to clean up.

Emptying yourself requires that you look at some things in your life that give you pain, but don't delve into your past without the help of the Holy Spirit.

God gave you the Holy Spirit for times such as these. In John 14:26, Jesus says that the Holy Spirit, also called Counselor, will teach you all things. The Apostle Paul says in 2 Corinthians 3:17, *"...where the Spirit of the Lord is, there is freedom." (NIV)*

When you empty yourself through the power of the Holy Spirit, you get counseling, comfort, guidance, teaching, and ultimately, freedom from negative thinking and behaviors related to your addiction.

The Many Faces of Sin

Sin is multifaceted. It can be blatant, but it also hides behind your traumas and can protect you for a time. For example, you probably put walls up over the years as people hurt, angered, or abused you. You may have found it necessary to hide your feelings, wear masks, or create false selves to face the world. But there's a price to pay for ungodly protection, beginning with a hardened heart and a depressed soul.

My mask caused me to be someone I was not. It also hardened my heart.

J **The Mask of Indifference**
   When I was a young girl, my sister, Sherry, and brother, Chuck, teased me mercilessly. Their goal was to get me to cry, which wasn't hard to do.

One day, my father took me aside and told me that if I quit crying, my siblings would quit teasing me. So the next time my brother and sister started to mock me, I put on a mask of indifference. When the tears started to well up, I smiled, walked away quietly, and cried in private. I did this over and over until the teasing stopped.

My dad's advice worked, so I used this coping method outside of the home. I put on a mask of indifference and independence to hide my vulnerable, sensitive side. I wore that mask for more than thirty-five years.

My mask caused me to be someone I was not. It also hardened my heart.

One of the walking wounded, I chose to date a rebel at age fourteen and by eighteen was married to him. Ten years later, I filed for divorce and became a single mother with three children, all under age four.

Having been deeply hurt by the relationship, I was even more determined to show the world I was tough. I put on a smile to hide the pain and continued wearing the mask of independence and indifference.

Three years later, I agreed to marry Jerry, but with one stipulation: He was never to use the "W" word. In other words, I didn't want to be called Wife because I associated it with suffering and oppression.

Jerry agreed and did a good job of avoiding the "W" word after we were married. Neither of us were Christians, so it seemed like a reasonable thing to do. Eventually, the wife word seeped its way into our relationship, but I never related to it, nor did I consider it an honor.

A few years after getting saved and baptized, I prayed and asked the Holy Spirit to help in understanding why I felt fake and separated from the rest of the world. The Holy Spirit showed me that it wasn't the world I was unattached to, it was God. I had long forgiven my siblings for the teasing, but Satan used the hurt of a little child to frame my thinking.

With the help of the Holy Spirit, I emptied the baggage of my life, including the lies that helped me to survive. It wasn't easy, but I said goodbye to the fake persona.

Miracles happened as I walked along The Solid Rock Road. For the first time in memory, I felt real and completely connected to God and other people. Getting back to myself gave me the joy I had been missing. I felt like a little girl who was finally allowed to twirl her skirt.

Today, my heart melts when Jerry calls me his wife. The "W" word is one of my most treasured. ∎

Getting Over Ourselves

We have to get over ourselves so we can get to God. The devil uses proven tricks to keep you from moving to the next level with God, and he's good at holding you back from your destiny. How many times have you sought God and began to experience positive changes and even miracles when all of a sudden, you start to question everything?

You begin to think negative thoughts, and say to yourself, "Who are you kidding? You're a loser and always will be. You're different from everyone else in church and no matter how hard you try, Christians will never accept or understand you. You're a fake and a liar. The only people who understand you are your old friends. You relate to them. They are like you and you are like them."

Any psychologist will tell you your addiction is talking. While that's a great recovery cliché, it's not a Christian reality. In truth, the devil is reconnecting you with your sin nature like a dog to its vomit, and urging you to wallow once again in your addiction like a pig in the mud.

Every time you allow old negative thoughts in, evil enters. When you choose to renew your mind and to think and act as the Bible instructs, you've emptied yourself of your sinful nature and can fill yourself up with the goodness of God.

So what does the devil whisper to you when no one else hears? It's important you identify the voice of Satan so you can filter out the trash he wants to pile on your mind.

Make a point of discerning the evil voices that keep feeding you garbage. Beware of any thoughts that make you think you don't belong in the Christian world. You must identify lies so you can live in the truth.

Satan likes to control all the voices in your head. He knows that what you think, you act out and become. The devil's words aren't new. They're so old you should be tired of them by now. But Satan uses the same tricks over and over because they have worked so far. He just keeps the never-ending tapes playing in your head so you can continue in your never-ending cycle of addiction-freedom-relapse.

Do the following exercise with the idea that you are identifying how the devil gets to you with lies that have become part of your belief system. The goal is to establish a belief system based on the Bible.

Carry your journal or a separate notebook around with you for one week. Keep it with you for seven straight days so you can write down the conversations you have with yourself. At the end of day seven, read your words aloud and see how much you live with negativity, temptation, self-loathing, insecurity, anger, pride, and other emotions.

Most importantly, make note of the patterns and identify the devil's words. If God is in your thoughts and you are in the Spirit, you will not be bitter at another person and you won't beat yourself up. When the devil speaks, he loves to condemn you and disconnect you from those who have your best interest at heart.

When you empty yourself of your sinful nature and internal condemnation, you are making room for God's truth, love, forgiveness, grace, and mercy. Satan wants us to be dogs who love vomit and pigs that are attracted to mud. But we don't have to live like that anymore.

8   The 'I'm Stupid' Tapes

Before I understood the power of God, I walked around as a continual victim. As a child, I believed I was stupid. In reality, I couldn't see three feet in front of me. I needed glasses, but no one knew it.

I couldn't clearly see characters on TV or the blackboard in school. Everyone was irritated by my ignorance, and I was embarrassed. The "I'm stupid" tapes began to play, then to replay automatically throughout my life—long after I got glasses at age eighteen.

The gang rape, followed by a series of bad relationships and poor choices, confirmed my stupidity. I no longer trusted myself to make reasonable decisions. During an eight-year relationship, my mate would literally grade me as a person and as a mother. According to him, I averaged a D-. At the time, I was grateful not to receive an F.

You may think I was stupid to continue the relationship, but you become what you think and what you say you are.

Your thoughts and words are powerful and that's why Satan uses them against you. My thoughts led me to an irrational belief system that I had to be perfect in every way to be okay. When that failed (only God is perfect), I became depressed and used drugs and alcohol to relieve the pressure. But that only added to the pressure and increased my shame.

During a discussion in a Solid Rock Road recovery group about the principle of emptying yourself and getting filled with the Holy Spirit, a male member commented that he felt like a freak his whole life. The other five group members each confessed to feeling like freaks too. When I admitted to experiencing the same alienation, God began to move in profound ways among the members because the secret was out and the evil behind the lie lost its power.

No one who calls on the name of Jesus is a freak. We are born again into the family of God. You just have to believe it. ■

Reveal Your Thoughts

You don't have to hide or hold onto anything that is ugly about yourself because if you do, you're feeding your sin nature. You might think that if you tell someone bad things you've done, or who you became in your addiction, they won't like you.

Most addicts feel judged by the straight world and by Christians in general. But that's judgment on your part. How will you know if people will accept you if you're not real with them in the first place? How can you be real with them if you deny the truth?

The main goal of this Principle is for you to acknowledge and release old concepts of who you are so you can begin living as a child of God. Galatians 5:24 says that those who belong to Christ have crucified the sinful nature. It's time to act like it.

When you've emptied your sinful self, the Holy Spirit will lead you to your rightful place in the kingdom of God. While Satan uses your uniqueness against you and makes you feel like a freak, God uses your gifts, talents, quirks, and individual personalities for His good.

 The following are questions worth thinking about. If you're using a journal, write down your thoughts and answers. If you don't like writing, mull the questions over in your mind.

- Who were you before you were wounded?
- What unique characteristics did God give you at birth or very early in life?
- What personalities have you taken on to survive painful situations?
- What attitudes do you hide behind?
- What are some of the negative scripts you keep playing out?
- What does the voice of the devil say to you, or about you?
- What does God say about you?

The most wonderful thing about being a Christian is being able to destroy the old script and play the role given to you by God before you were born. You can discover God's plan for your life when you use the mind of Christ and access the Holy Spirit. You must also make Jesus your Lord, not just your Savior.

Who is the Holy Spirit?

The Holy Spirit is your personal guide in your Christian walk. In John 14:16, Jesus tells the disciples He will be leaving (meaning crucified) but someone better will take His place. *"And I will ask the Father, and he will give you another Counselor to be with you forever." (NIV)*

That counselor is the Holy Spirit that lives in you from the point of salvation. Counseling from the Holy Spirit is divine. It's also free and available twenty-four hours a day. The Holy Spirit overpowers evil and is your source of strength, wisdom, and inspiration. When you are guided by the Holy Spirit, you will not return to your vomit or have the urge to wallow in the mud like a pig.

The problem we Christians have is that the Holy Spirit doesn't possess us. He doesn't just spring up and take over our life. We wish He would. It would make everything so much easier, and much better. Instead, the Holy Spirit lives in us, but waits for us to empower Him through surrender and the process of emptying ourselves.

In our sin nature, we're not that nice. When we're under the influence of the Holy Spirit, we're better to be around. As Galatians 5:22,23 explains: *"But the fruit of the Spirit is love, joy, peace, longsuffering, kindness, goodness, faithfulness, gentleness, self-control. Against such there is no law."*

The Bible also describes the Holy Spirit as the abiding guest (John 14:16), Spirit of truth (John 14:17), teacher (John 14:26), testifier (John 15:26), guide, voice of God, the Prophet (John 16:13), Glorifier of Jesus (John 16:14), witness to sonship (Romans

8:16), helper in prayer (Romans 8:26), and power to witness (Acts 1:8).

In Romans 8, Paul paints a beautiful picture of who we are with God. He confirms that we are not condemned, but rather protected by the power of the Holy Spirit to face adversities through His redeeming love. I suggest you read all of Romans 8 before proceeding with this chapter.

Romans 8:26 says that even when we don't know what to pray for, the Holy Spirit does and intercedes on our behalf. Obviously, the Holy Spirit knows us better than we know ourselves. Therefore, the Holy Spirit will lead you to your real Christian image, and He will help you change how you think, act, and even how you feel.

When the Holy Spirit protects and feeds your soul, you won't be so free to feed your addiction.

The Holy Spirit Lifestyle

We are born with a sin nature, but having been born again, we have been gifted with the Holy Spirit. Jesus referred to the Spirit of God as the power by which He cast out demons. If Jesus dealt with evil spirits on a daily basis, it makes sense that we do too. The difference is that Jesus automatically accessed the Holy Spirit while we often let our sinful nature control every aspect of our lives.

If what you feel isn't in line with the Word of God or wisdom from the Holy Spirit, you have to learn to forego your emotions. Living in the Spirit is a lifestyle change that takes time and practice.

The first step is to acknowledge and let go of your hurts. In order to do that, you have to think about events in your life that caused you pain, then let them go forever. When you clean out the dark parts of your heart, you can add more light.

You may be feeling fragile at the moment. After all, we have written a lot about the ugly side of human nature. We've used the vomit of dogs and pigs rolling in the mud to describe your propensity to abuse drugs and alcohol.

Let this be a reality check for you, not an offense. It's important you understand the spiritual battle at hand and your part in winning or losing.

In the following chapters, you'll learn how to arm yourself against the enemy for the ultimate victory. Keep reading, and don't give up minutes before the miracle. We've got faith in the work you've done and are about to do. We're standing with you in this battle because we are all part of the Army of God. We're in this together.

Anarchy would abound if all Christians determined right from wrong according to their own damaged and hardened hearts.

A Moral Guide

To win the battle, you need the mind of Christ and the Holy Spirit. If you rely on yourself, you're in trouble. While you have been transformed into God's love, your human heart is fickle and not always able to differentiate between right and wrong. In Jeremiah 17:9, God said *"the heart is deceitful above all things, and desperately wicked."*

It's true that your converted heart that is filled with the Holy Spirit can often identify deception. However, you still need a moral guide that can settle every matter for you. When you refer to the written Word of God, you are using a moral compass that will always keep you on the right path, going the right way.

Anarchy would abound if all Christians determined right from wrong according to their own damaged and hardened hearts. Therefore, you need a renewed heart that is transfixed on the finished work of Jesus Christ.

 We know you never planned on becoming a slave to addiction, but you do keep falling into old patterns of behavior and traps the devil sets. The following exercise will help you get to the bottom of this problem.

In Solid Rock Road groups, we help people identify their basic sin nature so they can kill it. Then we have a White Funeral to acknowledge we have buried it.

Answer the following questions. Some will have you thinking back to your childhood; some keep you in the present. But all of them require you to be 100 percent honest.

We urge you to complete this entire exercise and answer every single question. It may seem like a lot of work, but if you really want freedom, it is well worth your time and energy.

For those with a journal, get ready to write.

- In your earliest recollection, what did you do in secret?
- In your earliest recollection, what was your response to people hurting you? What were your thoughts and actions?
- In your earliest recollection, what were some of your negative thoughts towards your parents, siblings, friends, and teachers?
- In the last month, what did you do in secret?
- In the last month, what were some of your negative thoughts towards the people around you?
- When you are secretive, what are you protecting?
- In recent memory, what is your response to people hurting you – your thoughts and your actions?
- What was the first lie you ever told?
- What was the most recent lie you've told?
- When you lie, what are you protecting?
- In your earliest recollection, what made you sad?
- What makes you sad now?

- In your earliest recollection, what hurt your heart?
- What makes you angry now?
- What hurts you now?
- When you get the urge to use, what are the tapes that roll around in your head?
- What gives you permission or the go-ahead to use?

Excuses to Relapse

With a recovery ministry, we've heard it all. People blame their relapse on everything and everyone but themselves. Even when they admit they blew it, they justify their actions and blame-shift.

At a conference in Seattle, the speaker asked the audience what the opposite of learning was. We thought it out, but only came up with 'not learning.' But he said something that confirmed what we've been teaching. "The opposite of learning is blaming," he said. We looked at each other and in unison said, "Wow!"

When you blame others for your problems, you aren't learning the lesson God is trying to teach you. And since God never gives up on the lesson, you'll go around the same mountain a million times until He thinks you get it.

The following are some of the main excuses for relapse. Find yourself in one or more of these bullet points. When you identify an excuse you often use, determine that you will never use it again.

- No one will know. I can get away with it.
- No one really cares.
- I'm only hurting myself.
- My family and friends will forgive me in the end.
- God will forgive me, so why not?
- I'm bored and lonely.
- I'm hurt or angry and I'll show them.
- I can't stand the pain anymore.

- People are always hurting or burning me.
- I don't know what else to do.
- I can't help myself.
- I'm one of those people who just can't quit.
- I need to escape.
- I need one last fling and then it will be over.
- I've been good a long time so I deserve a good high.
- I need to remember how it feels to get high.
- Being a Christian is too hard.
- People are expecting way too much of me.
- I have too much pressure.

Killing the Lies

Your private thoughts cause most of your problems. You will never get free of your addictions if you keep secrets and never let anyone into your thought world.

It's ironic that addicts and those on the edge of relapse always protect lies in their mind and their sin nature. When you protect your sin nature, you find fault in others, get offended, and start shifting blame wherever you can. In most cases, your sin nature will attack the person who has been most willing to help you.

Consider the following scenario: You get counseling from a faithful Christian who is known for having wisdom. Though you agree with the advice at the time, your non-Christian thought process slowly takes over.

You start to obsess about the advice and without accessing the mind of Christ, convince yourself that the counselor was wrong, and you were misunderstood. You turn to non-Christians and tell them the problem. They give you advice according to the world, which to your non-Christian thought process makes complete sense.

Here's the reality of the situation: Your sin nature was exposed and in danger of extinction. To survive, your sin nature needed to regain control of your soul, which is your mind, will, and emotions. Your sin nature succeeded because you had yet to learn how to defend your faith, or to consistently use the spiritual life-saving techniques found in the Bible (and in this book).

Survival is a powerful instinct. Your sin nature will stop at nothing to live. You must stop at nothing to kill it. God won't do this for you, and the Holy Spirit will not force Himself on you. Your best chance of staying sober for a lifetime is to get in the habit of renewing your mind on a daily basis and empowering the Holy Spirit to do His work.

Exposing Evil

Picture standing under the light of God. Allow Him to expose the evil that lies dormant. When issues start to surface, acknowledge them and say goodbye out loud. For example, when we had a White Funeral at our last Solid Rock Road group, a member buried self pity.

"I lay you to rest," he said. "You are not going to have any more power over my future. You have allowed me to be a victim, and in turn to victimize others. Self pity, you have made me feel less valuable to God than others. You have made sure I was centered on myself and my needs. You have kept me from my destiny up to this point, but you are dead and Christ in me is alive. I choose to have faith and to trust that I am important to God and others. I am not a victim. I am victorious!"

When the participant identified his sin nature as self pity, he realized everything was filtered through the victim spirit. By the way, if you have the habit of thinking life isn't fair, you may have had some bad breaks, but that doesn't have anything to do with the way you're supposed to live as a Christian.

Fairness is relative. Is it fair that you are alive and others have died from their addictions? Is it fair that some people have had their children taken away by the state but yours have been with you throughout your addictions? Is it fair that some people get AIDS as a result of promiscuity, but you have tested negative? Is it fair that your boss hasn't fired you but so many other people are unemployed based on their personal choices?

Most importantly, is it fair that Jesus had to die for the sins of the world – including yours – when he was sinless?

If life was fair, you would probably suffer a lot more. You might also be dead.

Principle 3: Pray and Meditate on the Word of God Daily

"Watch and pray, lest you enter into temptation. The spirit indeed is willing, but the flesh is weak."
— Mark 14:38

When Christians say that their life sucks, our first two questions are, "Have you been reading the Bible and are you praying?" Ninety-nine percent of the time they answer, "No," or "Not as much as I used to," or "Not like I should."

Rarely has a tortured soul ready for relapse told us they were reading more, praying more, or meditating on the Word of God more than ever. Even if they said they were enmeshed in scripture twelve hours a day and praying the other twelve, we would know otherwise. Their negative attitude, growing level of fear, and signs of anger and blame-shifting would give them away. Yet, why is it that those on the edge of relapse usually deny their fragile condition, or defend themselves against people voicing concern?

After years of counseling people in The Solid Rock Road ministry, we have concluded that Christians in the recovery process continue to hide the truth. They have forgotten how to be genuine and are used to covering things up, making excuses, and explaining away realities. To be blunt, most people with addictive histories are liars.

Lying as a Habit

Lying is an addiction of its own and for some, it has become an art. Therefore, it can be as hard to overcome lying as it is to kick drugs and alcohol.

Chronic liars believe their lies protect them, get them out of trouble, and do them more good than harm. They tell lies to justify their actions and to make everyone believe they are strong in their Christian faith.

The Bible says that *all* liars are thrown into the lake of fire (Rev. 21:8). Not to scare you, but even if you are saved and go to church every day of the week, lying provides you with an opportunity to burn in hell with the devil. (We are aware of the "once saved, always saved" concept, but not convinced of it. And we certainly would never rely on it!)

Quit Lying

Never lie about the condition of your heart and mind. Don't lie when someone asks you how you are doing, or how your relationship with God is. If you've quit reading the Bible and praying, don't pretend you're doing devotionals, and no matter what, don't use the term "God said" if you haven't even spent time in His presence.

If you lie about these important aspects of your Christian life, you're not only a hypocrite, but are setting yourself up for relapse, not to mention a very hot and horrific future, if you know what we mean.

You don't have to make yourself look and sound better than you are. Your life is what it is. When you follow The Solid Rock Road and stay on the path of God, you won't have to make anything up ever again.

Living in the Truth

The goal of this chapter is to help you get in the habit of reading the Bible, praying, and meditating on the Word of God to discover and live in the truth, once and for all.

Let's start with the famous scripture in John 8:32: *"And you shall know the truth, and the truth shall make you free."*

For anyone with addiction issues, this is an important verse. And yet, to fully understand the intent of the author's heart, you should read the previous verse (John 3:31). *"...If you abide in My word, you are My disciples indeed."*

It's surprising how a two-letter word like "If" carries so much weight. But what this word means is that there are conditions you must meet in order to get the result described.

You can't live with a few jolts of the Holy Spirit on a Sunday morning. Your instructions are to search out scriptures for personal revelation.

Generally, the combination of the two sentences in John 8 means that truth won't just fall into your lap. Instead, you have to activate truth by consistently reading the Bible.

If you want to be set free from your addictions, or to maintain the freedom you've received, you are responsible to discover and live in the truth. You can't depend on the information or even the inspiration you get from a meeting, a sermon, or a song. You can't live with a few jolts of the Holy Spirit on a Sunday morning. Your godly instructions are to search out the scriptures for personal revelation.

No one can take your journey of discovery for you, although I'm sure people who love you have tried. There's nothing quite like a good co-dependent to take co-ownership of your issues—to constantly try and save you from your self-destructive habits.

These people will lead you in Bible studies, buy you devotionals and read them to you, pray in your place, schedule and reschedule appointments with your pastor or counselor, drive you to your meetings to make sure you go, make excuses for your behaviors, and do a million other things to get you the help they have determined you need.

In turn, you resent being watched like a hawk and being told how to live. Often, you use their co-dependent behavior as another excuse to get angry or frustrated enough to abuse your favorite substance.

When we counsel spouses, children, and other family members of an active substance abuser, we always tell them, "Never work harder than the addict."

Setting Boundaries

Like most counselors, we work with families of the addicted to help them set boundaries and deal with their issues of co-dependency. This makes us mad because it's not right that addiction entangles loved ones, causing them to need counseling and freedom.

We're not surprised that co-dependents are willing to face the truth and get their behavior under control. After all, their job is to fix everything. Meanwhile, you the addict, do everything possible to resist change and interrupt the process. You do the bare minimum to say you've tried and get everyone off your back.

Your manipulations are often successful because those who love you are desperate to see their prayers answered and efforts rewarded. They see what they want to see, and in many cases, they see what *you* want them to see.

While we were addicts, we have also spent many years as co-dependents. We have first-hand experience with how the game is played. And to be truly honest, we're still not immune to co-dependent behaviors.

Defining Co-Dependency

We use the term 'co-dependent' because it's a universally accepted term. The National Mental Health Association describes co-dependency as "a learned behavior that can be passed down from one generation to another. It is an emotional and behavioral condition that affects an individual's ability to have a healthy, mutually satisfying relationship. It is also known as 'relationship addiction' because people with co-dependency often form or maintain relationships that are one-sided, emotionally destructive, and/or abusive."

In actuality, co-dependency is a sin and those practicing it must repent and use the Word of God to overcome this tendency. When we step in front of God because we think we can help, we block God's way and eliminate Him from the process.

God won't fight anyone for position. He'll just wait for us to get sick and tired of working on our loved ones to the point of personal exhaustion. When we finally surrender, God steps in and does what we could never do.

Generally, God says to take responsibility for our own actions. If you're an addict, it's time to gather up all your own stuff and deal with it.

If you're a co-dependent who has worked harder on your loved one's sobriety than he or she has, it's time to gather up everything that's not yours, and give it back!

 If you truly want to stay clean and sober for the rest of your life, you need to identify people who have become co-dependent on your behalf. You have to release them.

Set your loved ones free from *your* addictions. Tell them they don't have to do the work anymore. Let them know you are going to surrender, empty yourself of your sinful nature, and study the Word of God.

Make an appointment with all your co-dependents and read them the following list of bullet points. Feel free to add to this list, but don't leave any out of your conversation.

- I am responsible for my Christianity and sobriety.
- I appreciate everything you've ever done for me, but I have to discover God's truth for myself.
- Pray for me, but don't pray in my place.
- Let me either earn your trust or prove I'm untrustworthy.
- When I mess up, tell everyone the absolute truth.
- Allow me to deal with *all* the consequences of my addiction or relapse.
- Be consistent. When you make a threat, follow through on it.
- If I ask for your help, you have my permission to say 'No.'
- If you think I'm lying, call me on it.

Complete the Assignment

As we write this, we're wondering how many of you are unselfish enough to complete the assignment. If you can't have this conversation, we question your long-term sobriety and your commitment to taking responsibility for your life and your Christian walk.

No one knows you have been given this assignment, so what your friends and family don't know won't hurt them, right? Well, what they don't know may not hurt them, but keeping silent will definitely hurt you.

For the Co-Dependent
If you're reading this book because someone you love is addicted and you have identified some co-dependent tendencies in yourself, the above bullets are useful for you too. You should initiate the same kind of conversation with the addict in your life, using the following revised bullets. Make an appointment and be very clear about your objectives. Tell your loved one that you will no longer work to control their addiction and that you're surrendering them to God. Also let them know the following:

- You are responsible for your own Christianity and sobriety.
- I'm sure you appreciate everything I've done for you, but I have to get out of the way so you can discover God's truth on your own.
- I'll pray for you, but I won't pray in place of you.
- At this point, it's your responsibility to earn my trust or to prove you are untrustworthy.
- When you mess up, I'm going to tell everyone the absolute truth.
- I won't make excuses for you. Instead, I'm going to allow you to deal with *all* the consequences of your addiction and/or relapse.
- I'm going to be consistent. When I make a threat, know that I plan to follow through on it.
- If you ask for help, I have the right to say 'No.'
- If I think you're lying, I will tell you.

If you can't sit with the addict in your life and have this conversation, then your cycle of co-dependency will continue. Worse, you'll continue to be in the way of

God. We suggest you say the Surrender prayer, take your loved one to the cross, and leave them there. Put them in God's hands.

> What Jerry learned was that the only way to elevate his mind beyond human capacity was to use God as his intellectual resource.

The Habit of Christianity

We're convinced that starting a routine of daily reading, prayer, and meditation is the single most important step you can take toward long-term peace and freedom from addictions. So we're taking this opportunity to help you get in the habit of reading the Bible and allowing the Word of God to penetrate your soul and teach you things you didn't know.

In our Solid Rock Road groups, Jerry (our director and Jamee's husband) always shares his story about reading the Bible for the first time. He says it was like reading a book written in a foreign language. He didn't understand a word of it and didn't think he ever would.

Even so, Jerry began attending Bible college within the first four months of being born again. The challenge to read and understand became a source of fear and frustration for him. But he didn't give up.

What Jerry learned was that the only way to elevate his mind beyond human capacity was to use God as his intellectual resource, so he invited the Holy Spirit to do the thinking for him. Over time, Jerry's comprehension increased and his love for the Word of God blossomed. In our Solid Rock Road groups, Jerry uses his experiences to encourage participants to read whether they understand what is written or not.

To get more of the Word, we suggest everyone get a version of the Bible that is easier to read than the Old King James. If you're not sure which version will work for you, ask other Christians if they can recommend a Bible translation that provides more user-friendly language. For example, New King James, New International Version, and the New Living Translation are excellent resources and will help you more easily interpret the scriptures. You can also use The Message, which is the Bible in contemporary language.

If you get into the habit of reading the Bible, you are opening the door to knowledge and wisdom. If you have never read the Bible in its entirety, it would be a good idea to use a reading plan that will take you through the entire book in one year.

People often make the mistake of starting in Genesis and try to read the Bible like they would a novel, from beginning to end. If this has never worked for you, then the reading plan may be your answer.

By the way, The Solid Rock Road team believes in reading the Bible all the way through. If you don't have a printed copy of such a plan, you can get one from the Internet. One resource is Biblegateway.com.

If the thought of reading the Bible in its entirety overwhelms you, start with the book of John in the New Testament and read Proverbs from the Old Testament.

You are What You Take In

Doctors and nutritionists often say, "You are what you eat." In the Christian realm, you are what you read and think about.

For example, if you view pornography regularly, you will think about sex more than is natural. Anyone caught up in sexual addiction has the same problem as a drug addict; they meditate on their lust and it results in compulsive, obsessive behavior.

Therefore, if you want to consistently overcome your addictions, you must replace your lustful thoughts with pure thoughts. Now that's a challenge for many. Some people think it's impossible to train their brain to think pure thoughts. But the Bible says we can do all things through Christ. And it says to meditate on whatever is pure.

When we think about purification in the physical sense, we visualize a filtering system. Many homes use water purifiers to remove contaminates such as parasites, bacteria, and toxic metals.

To the natural eye, tap water appears fine, but pollutants quickly materialize under a microscope. Even natural springs, considered safe and contaminant-free in the 1800s, must now be tested and oftentimes treated because pollutants have seeped into the nation's groundwater over time.

The same is true for our minds.

Protecting the Mind
Although sin has existed since Adam and Eve ate the forbidden fruit, there is evidence that impurity has evolved to dangerous levels in today's world. It's going to get worse before it gets better, so it's essential that you install and turn on spiritual filters in your mind and heart.

Today, you don't have to go to a strip club to view naked women, you just have to turn on your computer or the television and channel surf. A few years ago, the x-rated programming came on in the wee hours of the morning. Now you can see naked people any time of the day.

Sex is the subject of many primetime television shows. Kids are watching, but instead of being shocked, they are numb to impurity. Some even mimic the look and actions of Hollywood role models who have forgotten their morals.

We don't believe such conditioning of our minds happens by accident. The devil and the unsaved have used the media to modify our behaviors and make immorality the norm. Basically, we're being trained like circus animals to conform and perform in the present culture. It may be pleasing to the crowds, but behind the scenes, we are fed the meat of compromise day in and day out. Meanwhile, we get more contaminated and our appetite for the world and its ways grows.

 We want you to understand the battle you face. Staying sober for a lifetime requires a change in your lifestyle, and a new way of seeing the world.

First, you must see the world as it really is. This is hard to do when you're so enmeshed in modern culture, but absolutely necessary to live the Christian lifestyle.

The following exercise will get you started:

1. Write down all the sexual content that appears within the television programs you watch.
2. Pay attention to the commercials and write down all the sexual innuendos.
3. Listen to the lyrics of the songs you hear and write down all the references to sex.
4. Take note of the articles about sex and the ads about sex in the magazines you read.
5. How many times has your online in-box tempted you to open a message or web page that promotes sex? Have you been tempted? Did you click?
6. When channel surfing, how many television channels offer naked or nearly naked images?

The Media

Overt sexuality and all forms of sin are in your face all day long. But what about God? How often does the world ask you to think about Him and what He says about your life? Compare the promotion of sex against the promotion of God and you will see that the fight for purity is an uphill battle.

By the way, the media not only promotes sex, but is guilty of promoting alcohol to your children. Shows and commercials make drinking appear glamorous, refreshing, and culturally acceptable. Can you imagine a Budweiser commercial showing drunken people fighting outside a bar, or a drunk driver killing an innocent child? It just won't happen. Fantasy supersedes reality when it comes to advertising.

Over the past several years, a series of TV commercials has promoted the use of prescription drugs. This seems innocent enough, but you and your children are being indoctrinated into the pop-a-pill culture that is ruining a lot of lives – maybe even yours.

Don't minimize the abuse of prescription medication. Prescription drugs are as dangerous as street drugs as far as we're concerned. In our ministry, we often have more success getting people free from methamphetamines than we do with those addicted to Methadone, Vicodin and other pain killers. And we've seen more people die from an overdose of prescription medication than heroine or methamphetamines.

Meditation

What you think about, or what you obsess about, is your meditation. If you're an addict, you meditate on the substances you abuse. Since you can hardly think of anything else, your addiction becomes you.

With your thoughts dedicated to your next high, there's little room for family and friends, and even less room for God. This is the opposite of how Christians are to live. God is supposed to be first. You should think of Him when you open our eyes in the morning, throughout the day, and right before you go to sleep.

Both God and Satan want your meditation. Neither can force you into thinking one way or another. It's your choice and one of the many battles you face in your recovery process.

Philippians 4:8 offers great advice on the subject. *"Finally, brethren, whatever things are true, whatever things are noble, whatever things are just, whatever things are pure, whatever things are lovely, whatever things are of good report, if there is any virtue and if there is anything praiseworthy—meditate on these things."*

Read and think about the following scriptures. There's a lot of negativity attached to addictions, so you need the Word of God to counteract your thoughts and become your new filter. You must know what God says about you, and claim it.

- I am a child of God. (John 1:12)
- I am part of the true vine. (John 15:1-5)
- I am Christ's friend. (John 15:15)
- I am chosen by Christ to bear His fruit. (John 15:16)
- I am a child of God; God is spiritually my Father. (Romans 8:14-15; Galatians 3:26; 4:6)
- I am a joint heir with Christ, sharing His inheritance with Him. (Romans 8:17)
- I am a temple—a dwelling place—of God. His Spirit and His life dwell in me. (1 Corinthians 3:16; 6:19)
- I am united to the Lord and am one spirit with Him. (1 Corinthians 6:17)
- I am a member of Christ's body. (1 Corinthians 12:27; Ephesians 5:30)
- I am a new creation. (2 Corinthians 5:17)
- I am reconciled to God and a minister of reconciliation. (2 Corinthians 5:18-19)
- I am a saint. (Ephesians 1:1; 1 Corinthians 1:2; Philippians 1:1; Colossians 1:2)
- I am God's workmanship—His handiwork—born anew in Christ to do His work. (Ephesians 2:10)

- I am a fellow citizen with God's Family. (Ephesians 2:19)
- I am righteous and holy. (Ephesians 4:24)
- I am a citizen of heaven, seated in heaven right now. (Philippians 3:20; Ephesians 2:6)
- I am hidden with Christ in God. (Colossians 3:4)
- I am an expression of the life of Christ because He is my life. (Colossians 3:4)
- I am chosen of God, holy and dearly loved. (Colossians 3:12; 1 Thessalonians 1:4)
- I am a holy partaker of a heavenly calling. (Hebrews 3:1)
- I am a partaker of Christ; I share in His life. (Hebrews 3:14)
- I am one of God's living stones, being built up in Christ as a spiritual house. (1 Peter 2:5)
- I am a member of a chosen race, a royal priesthood, a holy nation, a people for God's own possession. (1 Peter 2:10)
- I am an enemy of the devil. (1 Peter 5:8)
- I am a child of God and I will resemble Christ when He returns. (1 John 3:1-2)
- I am born of God, and the evil one—the devil— cannot touch me. (1 John 5:18)
- I died with Christ and died to the power of sin's rule over my life. (Romans 6:1-6)
- I am free forever from the condemnation. (Romans 8:1)
- I have received the Spirit of God into my life that I might know the things freely given to me by God. (1 Corinthians 2:12)
- I have been given the mind of Christ. (1 Corinthians 2:16)
- I have been bought with a price, I am not my own; I belong to God. (1 Corinthians 6:19-20)
- Since I have died, I no longer live for myself, but for Christ. (2 Corinthians 5:14-15)

- I have been crucified with Christ, and it is no longer I who live, but Christ lives in me. The life I am now living is Christ's life. (Galatians 2:20)
- I was chosen in Christ to be holy before the foundation of the world. I am without blame before Him. (Ephesians 1:4)
- I have direct access to God through the Spirit. (Ephesians 2:18)
- I have been rescued from the domain of Satan's rule and transferred to the Kingdom of Christ. (Colossians 1:13)
- I have been justified—completely forgiven and made righteous. (Romans 5:1)

The Mind of Christ

This book is more raw truth than gentle persuasion. As you read on, you may even feel like Mercurochrome is being poured into your wounds. This may make you uncomfortable, and it will probably be painful, but healing takes place when antiseptic is allowed to do its cleansing work. For Christians, the antiseptic is the blood of Jesus that cleanses us from all evil.

Our goal is to help you understand the beauty and grace of God. And while God is love, the Bible describes the Word of God as a sword, a hammer, and a fire. It cuts, it clobbers, and burns. That's not exactly gentle, but that's often what it takes to destroy the lies and tricks of the devil.

We take the Bible very personally, believing that every word was written for us. When we pray, we don't doubt that God is listening intently, ready to respond with an exhortation, a sign, scripture, symbol, word of truth, or some form of imagery. And some of our favorite moments are when we're contemplating something we've seen or heard from God or about God, getting insight into our lives, and getting inspiration for others.

You know you should read the Bible, think about what it says, and pray to God. But what you may not understand is that all three of these actions must be performed to stay fully connected with God, who is your source of life and energy.

This connection allows truth to penetrate your soul and your spirit to rise above your sin nature. When you disconnect from God, you are in human default mode. This means that you are being directed by your inner voice, which has gotten you into trouble your whole life.

> **Your inner voice wants to protect your sin nature and will war against the truth of God.**

We don't have to remind you what your sin nature looks like. You got a heavy dose of reality in Principle 2. But what about that inner voice of yours that keeps reciting old news, has a tendency to obsess over negative events in your life, and loves to send you places well off God's beaten path? What does it tell you and how does that voice affect your relationship with God, yourself, and others?

We have to fight against the voice of Satan who wants to minimize our ministry. We often hear that there is no hope in the world, that all our efforts are futile, and that no one is ever going to get this message and take it to heart.

Our inner voices whisper sweet nothings, such as, "Who do you think you are to write about the things of God?" It says a lot of things that are hurtful and make us doubt, fear, and become frustrated. But we have learned to silence those voices and listen intently to the voice of God. You can do the same, though it does take some practice.

Whose Voice is It?

Psychologists, psychiatrists, as well as New Age philosophers insist that our inner voice knows the truth and will give us all the answers we need. But this can be dangerous because our inner voice is directed through self-will. It filters through past experiences and the world system.

Your inner voice wants to protect your sin nature and will actually war against the truth of God.

Even small decisions can have a major impact on Your Christian life.

Christians get in trouble when they believe they are hearing God but it's their own inner voice coming through loud and clear. This may make you insecure about whether you are divinely inspired or not, but there is a system you can use to make sure that what you are hearing is truth.

First, check it against Biblical instruction. Second, get in the habit of seeking counsel from your leaders. Even small decisions can have a major impact on your Christian life.

Proverbs 11:14 says, *"Where no counsel is, the people fall: but in the multitude of counsellors there is safety."* *(KJV)* To prove this point, Solomon writes something very familiar in Proverbs 15:22, *"Without counsel, plans go awry, but in the multitude of counselors they are established."*

The best advice we can give you is, leave nothing to chance. When you are making decisions, don't get prideful and religious; get guidance. Most importantly, if several wise people agree on an answer, take their advice. This may mean that you have to do something you don't want to do, or you can't do something you want to do. At first, you'll hate this accountability process, but I guarantee you will totally love the long-term results.

In the Stay Accountable chapter, we provide stories of people who resisted doing their own thing and became living testimonies to the power of fellowship and obedience. We also tell about the destruction of those who retained their independence and insisted on doing their own thing.

Christianity is an unchaning reality that refuses to be minimized or distorted.

Preserving Christianity

Christianity carries age-old thought into our modern-day world. It was never intended to conform to cultural attitudes or to change with time. Christianity is an unchanging reality that refuses to be minimized or distorted. Therefore, our premise is that you can't mix New Age ideologies with the laws of God. And yet, people try to do it all the time, including many Christians.

Christianity as described in the Bible is pure so any time you add or take away from it, you end up with impurity. If you're painting your wall white, what happens when you mix even a small amount of brown? It is no longer white, it is beige. If you remove the red tint from the color orange, you are left with yellow.

You can't add or subtract from any color or it changes the color completely. The same is true for the Bible. Many religions and philosophies believe the Bible in part and incorporate some teachings into their spiritual thesis. Others add to the Bible or even change it.

Unfortunately, many people add and take away from the Bible to create their own view of God and to justify their actions. Some people actually believe they are God, or have a revelation of God that is different from the Bible, or is an extension of it. This is not true because the Bible warns about false teachers who preach contrary to Jesus.

New Age Definition

To get an objective point of view on New Age philosophies, we accessed Wikipedia. We had no idea that this free online dictionary would make a better point than we ever could about the anti-Christ spirit of New Ageism. Therefore, we are including portions of Wikipedia's definition.

To ensure you don't get confused by our opinions and the words written in Wikipedia, we have indented the dictionary's essay.

> "The term New Age describes a broad movement of late 20th century and contemporary Western culture, characterized by an individual eclectic approach to spiritual exploration.
>
> Many ideas of the New Age movement are elements of older spiritual and religious traditions, from both east and west, melded with modern ideas from science, especially psychology and ecology.
>
> Though there are no formal or definitive boundaries for membership, those who are likely to sample many diverse teachings and practices (from both 'mainstream' and 'fringe' traditions) and to formulate their own beliefs and practices based on their experiences can be considered as New Age.
>
> Rather than following the lead of an organized religion, 'New Agers' typically construct their own spiritual journey based on material taken as needed from the mystical traditions of the world's religions,

including shamanism, neopaganism and occultism.

The term *New Age* is generally limited to Western or modern context where the Judeo-Christian tradition and/or Positivism are dominant, so the use of "alternative" in New Age thought generally implies a contrast with these dominant religious and/or scientific beliefs. Hence, many New Age ideas and practices contain either explicit or implied critiques of organized mainstream Christianity."

There's more included in this Wikipedia definition, but you get the idea.

New Ageism Versus Christianity

New Age teaches that humans are basically good and its philosophies center on religious tolerance and moral diversity. Christianity teaches that our nature is to sin and we must overcome our natural propensity to defy God.

While Christianity promotes absolute truth that cuts to the heart and causes conviction, New Ageism promotes relative truth, acceptance, and tolerance.

The following chart reveals significant differences between Christianity and New Age theologies. This is an incomplete list, but provides you with an at-a-glance view of the path that God has set according to Biblical principles.

Everyone is entitled to choose their religious beliefs. If you are a Christian, you have made the choice to follow the narrow path that God has created.

Are you on the narrow path or have you veered off? Use the following illustration to answer this very important question.

Christianity	New Age Ideologies
God is the center	Humans are the center
A single path leads to God	Many roads lead to God
Truth (Word) sets us free	Truth is relative
Restricted to teachings in the Bible	Infuses modern thoughts of science, psychology, ecology
Must be saved to become a believer	No defined boundaries of membership
Stresses purity of the Word of God	Blends traditions & religions such as shamanism, neopaganism, and occultism
Exposes and eliminates the sin nature	Self-acceptance and self-love: humans are basically good
God holds and gives out the power	The human mind has deep levels and vast powers
Involves meditation on God's Word and rebukes idols	Involves meditation without traditional religious beliefs
Encourages spiritual exploration in the Bible	Encourages spiritual exploration not in the Bible
Love for God and others	Love for self & feeling good
Stresses the importance of God's limitations	Opposed to the narrow-mindedness of Christianity
God is king	No centralized hierarchy
There is one God and you are not it	Main doctrines are Evolutionary Godhead – humans will become gods
Jesus rose from the dead, fulfilled hundreds of prophecies	False prophets died and are only written about
Offers godly power	Offers power from within or through the demonic
One death followed by either eternal heaven or hell	Afterlife doesn't punish, it teaches
Faith in God's plans	You create your own reality
Belief in sowing and reaping	Belief in karma
One written system of belief	A hodge-podge of beliefs

8 New Age Experience

While walking through the city of Capitola (near Santa Cruz), a woman jumped down from a cement wall that separated the sidewalk from the beach and exclaimed, "You are in danger! You must leave immediately. Head west!" Having identified herself as a psychic, she told me someone evil was running after me and that my only hope of escape was to get out of town.

Having recently learned that my live-in boyfriend and business partner of eight years had molested my daughter, fear gripped me. While many of these horrible, dark days are still fuzzy, I do remember thinking that God had put the psychic in my path.

That night, I was on a plane to Hawaii with a friend. My daughters were safely stashed at my parents' house and I had gathered up some money to keep me afloat for however long I needed to stay away.

After landing on the island, some nice people introduced themselves to me and my friend, then offered to guide us to a spiritual center. I had only been saved a few weeks, so I truly believed God had not only spoken through the psychic, but also led me to Hawaii and into the hands of friendly strangers.

I spent three weeks in Hawaii, learning the basic principles of *A Course in Miracles*. The teachers and students talked a lot about God and Jesus, so at first I was completely immersed in the concepts and thrilled by the possibility that I could live in a miracle state. I had hope that I could create a new reality, especially after enduring such great suffering at home.

Soon after, I began to get uncomfortable with what they said was 'channeled' by Jesus to the author of the *Course*. Though I didn't know much about the Bible, I sensed the teachings were false. For example, *Course* leaders claimed that Jesus was used to demonstrate the illusion that man was still in heaven and sin and death weren't real. They taught that man thinks he is separated from God through his own ego and mistaken beliefs. By undoing the death reality, *Course* gurus claimed we can undo sin and come to the realization that there is no actual separation from God.

And yet, at home, a wicked man with evil intentions had sinned against my daughter in the most vile acts a grown man can do. I wondered how heaven could tolerate housing such a defiled human being, and I knew in my heart that God had created hell for people like my daughter's molester.

People love the idea that miracles can happen without obedience to the Word. But they can't.

As much as I wanted to believe the island speakers and teachers, I couldn't buy their truth. I did remain pleasant and participated in some of the exercises, which I later renounced.

Though the *Course* people asked me to stay longer and even agreed to house my children if I sent for them, I was eager to get home. However, my good friend got caught up in the teachings so she stayed. I never heard from her again.

The philosophy of the *Course* contains theological elements from Christianity, Eastern mysticism, psychology, and New Age spirituality. Its female author was a clinical psychologist by training who was assisted in writing the *Course* by a psychologist friend.

Why would millions of people all over the world believe this woman had all the answers to life's questions? When I think back on that experience in Hawaii, I realize that people were searching for a way to remove personal responsibility, especially regarding sin.

People love the idea that miracles can happen without obedience to God's Word. But they can't. Still, they prefer to feel good, believe unproven ideas, and ignore the fact that judgment will come with only two possibilities: heaven or hell. ■

10 Principles as Inspiration

You may wonder if the 10 Principles of The Solid Rock Road are of God, especially since we say that the Holy Spirit inspired them. We believe they are because they line up with the Bible.

We used the Bible as our study guide, our source for insight, and to support the Principles. Along the way, we received revelation through the Word of God to help explain concepts.

For example, when we began to write this chapter, we didn't plan to include the concept of New Ageism. But as we started to express the importance of truth, we realized we had to illustrate how Satan creates and uses lies to get people off The Solid Rock Road and onto the Yellow Brick Road.

Then we remembered the psychic. Looking back, we see that she really did have insight, but her source was not from God. Satan used Sherry's vulnerability as an opportunity to steer a newborn spiritual baby in the wrong direction. What appeared to be a divinely inspired intervention at the Capitola wall was in reality a demonic interruption. If Sherry had been connected to a church body, she might have received a warning or words of wisdom from her pastor or leader.

Still, God protected Sherry in Hawaii and the Holy Spirit helped separate truth from lies. She escaped the snare.

If you're wondering about theology or philosophy you have believed or been introduced to, compare it with the teachings of the Bible. If you are still not sure about it, ask your pastor or a strong Christian leader to check it out.

If you have New Age or cult materials in your home, you would be wise to get rid of it and to renounce its teachings.

Beware of False Prophets

There are ways to know if someone is practicing New Age philosophies or true Christianity. First John 4:1-3 gives us a good start:

"Beloved, do not believe every spirit, but test the spirits, whether they are of God; because many false prophets have gone out into the world. By this you know the Spirit of God: Every spirit that confesses that Jesus Christ has come in the flesh is of God, and every spirit that does not confess that Jesus Christ has come in the flesh is not of God."

The *Course* almost got away with following scripture because it acknowledges Jesus, but then it teaches the following: "The name of Jesus is the name of the one who was a man but saw the face of Christ in all his brothers and remembered God. So he became identified with Christ, a man no longer, but at one with God. The man was an illusion, for he seemed to be a separate being, walking by himself, within a body that appeared to hold his self from Self, as all illusions do."

If you never feel convicted of the sins you've committed, you will continue in them.

We suggest using 1 John 4:1-3 as a filter so you can differentiate between the divine and the demonic. Yet many Christians are easily fooled because they don't hold the Bible as their only source of truth, they don't understand the laws or heart of God, nor have they practiced listening in order to hear His voice.

Many people are self-indulgent, tending to make decisions based on emotions, wants, and instant gratification rather than what is right or what God and people with wisdom would suggest for a greater, long-term reward.

In our experiences, the biggest problem is that people are drawn to ideas and thoughts that get them off the spiritual hook, and they want to hear what they want to hear. This is why many addicts feel better in grace-oriented churches. They want to hear that God forgives and that all is well in their world.

If you have a hard time hearing the truth and tend to tune it out, we suggest you fight your flesh in order to listen. Attend church where purity is not only taught but also practiced. Insist on going no matter how uncomfortable or convicted you feel.

If you never feel convicted for the sins you've committed, you will continue in them. This includes your sin of addiction.

There's a major difference between conviction and condemnation. The Holy Spirit brings conviction, which will cause you to change. The devil promotes condemnation, which results in your feelings of guilt and shame, but has no power to help you change.

The grace message is one of the most beautiful truths in the Bible, but it is not the only truth. Yes, God forgives you of your sins when you repent, but there are many scriptures that describe a state of apostasy in which the hand of God is permanently removed from someone's life. We're not sure where God draws the line, we just know He does.

Satan Knows History

Satan walked the earth before Adam and Eve were created, so he knows the planet's entire history. The evil spirits that have been assigned to you since birth know your entire history, including every major trauma and disappointment you've had. They are good at reminding you about all your wrong choices, and the people who did you wrong.

One of Satan's jobs is to get you and others off the path of righteousness. You'll learn more about that later in the book, but for now, learn to be cautious of falling into New Age philosophies or any other non-Biblical ideologies.

If you lean toward New Age thinking or are associated with a group that has a Christian slant with theologies outside Biblical truth, get into prayer and ask God for the truth. Then start reading the Bible every day.

Non-Christian Beliefs

Many famous people model non-Christian beliefs. In Hollywood, Tom Cruise and John Travolta promote Scientology, a New Age religion based on L. Ron Hubbard's personal theories, born out of psychology and science.

Hubbard says, "Man is an immortal, spiritual being. His experience extends well beyond a single lifetime. His capabilities are unlimited, even if not presently realized—and those capabilities *can* be realized. He is able to not only solve his own problems, accomplish his goals and gain lasting happiness, but also achieve new, higher states of awareness and ability."

There's no room for God in Scientology. According to Hubbard, we can solve our own problems and live several lives. His philosophy was derived through the combined teachings of his own mind, Sigmund Freud, a Native American medicine man, a Beijing magician, Buddhist monks, and the study of physics and other sciences.

In our observation, New Age philosophers like Hubbard steer very clear of scripture or take a few Biblical truths to call their own. And like all good New Agers, Hubbard's concepts are based on "improved understanding of his fundamental nature: that man is basically good and it is pain, suffering, and loss that lead him astray."

This is the opposite of what the Bible says. Therefore, the study of Scientology is a Yellow Brick Road.

It's totally ironic that New Agers refuse to believe that there is a heaven and hell, especially in light of Revelation 19:19-20, which reads, *"Then I saw the beast, the kings of the earth, and their armies, gathered together to make war against Him who sat on the horse and against His army. Then the beast was captured, and with him the false prophet who worked signs in his presence, by which he deceived those who received the mark of the beast and those who worshiped his image. These two were cast alive into the lake of fire burning with brimstone."*

Ironically, New Agers who deny the hell experiences are the ones who are destined to burn in the lake of fire.

Keeping the Devil at a Distance

Only God can read your mind. Satan can't. However, he can manipulate you through fears and questions he knows you have. All Satan has to do is watch your reactions, observe your body language, and listen to what you say. Since Satan knows the Bible backward and forward, he uses Luke 6:45 to make plans: *"For out of the abundance of the heart his mouth speaks."*

> **The devil will stop at nothing to make sure you are fully tempted, to the point where you give in, and say out loud, "I can't resist."**

Therefore, you must quickly get a lot of God and His Word planted in your heart. That way, words you speak will repel the devil instead of drawing him to you. When you talk to God, use words of faith, and claim scripture out loud, Satan stays away.

On the other hand, if you whine about your problems and if you doubt out loud, you can be sure that the devil's ears perk right up and the evil spirits get to work reviving your sin nature and self-will.

When the devil hears you talk about your addictions and how weak you are feeling, he will put a drug dealer in your path or have old friends drop by with a twelve-pack of your favorite beer to further weaken your resolve. The devil will stop at nothing to ensure you are fully tempted, to the point where you give in and say out loud, "I can't resist."

He will also use tactics to tempt you when you're at your best and in tune with God. The difference is that when you have been reading the Word and spending time with God, you are spiritually empowered, you are prepared for the spiritual battle, and have the Word of God as your weapon.

If your sin nature and self-will are allowed to dominate, you are destined for trouble. Pride and self-will prevent you from seeking Christian counsel. And you'll resist talking to people who might say no to your ungodly ideas and plans. Instead, when you're in a funk, you prefer to share your thoughts with those you know will agree with your negativity and not judge you.

If you want your life to be great, find someone whose life is already great and do what they do. Don't let your personal experiences dictate your future. Instead, design your life by finding Christians whose footsteps you can follow.

The Word

While it's important to trust God, you should also take steps to understand His words. God made sure the Bible was written so we would know right from wrong and have every solution to life's problems at our fingertips. And like a good father, He expects us to grow up, make good choices, and live a blessed life.

Never forget that the Word of God is your compass, as described in Deuteronomy 8:3: "...*man shall not live by bread alone; but man lives by every word that proceeds from the mouth of the LORD."*

In Matthew 4:4, Jesus used Old Testament scripture to resist Satan's temptation. If Jesus had to use the Word of God, wouldn't you be wise to do the same?

> ### When you use the sword of the Spirit against Satan, he can't even fight back. You win, hands down.

Use the Sword of the Spirit

In a later chapter, you will learn how to protect yourself against the wiles of the devil using the armor of God. We also write about the sword of the Spirit, which is the Word of God. This means you have a weapon to cut through lies and defeat the devil.

According to John 8:44, the devil is the father of lies. There isn't an ounce of truth in him. He is good at whispering lies that seem like truth into our itching spiritual ears. He likes it when we think outside the Biblical box.

You need the armor, but the armor is mostly used to defend yourself against your enemy. You need the sword, which is the Word. With it, you will not be fencing with the devil, you will be slaughtering him.

If you've watched any swashbuckler movies, you've seen metal against metal as the good and bad guys battle it out with their swords. But when you use the sword of the Spirit against Satan, he can't even fight back. You win, hands down.

Turn the tables on the devil. When he says you're not going to make it, or you don't measure up, or you're a loser and an addict who can never quit for good, call him a liar, then thrash him with scripture. He may come at you from another angle, but if you're ready with the Word of God at all times, he can come from behind, from above, from anywhere and you can instantly take him out.

Prayer: The Hour that Changed the World

Your life will change dramatically when you have an ongoing, personal relationship with God. You have to spend time with God if you want to know Him – the same way you got to know your best friend or your spouse. Friendships and marriage are the result of establishing and maintaining intimate relationships.

You can't expect to have intimacy if you keep your distance from God, or if you perceive He is estranged from you. James 4:8 says, *"Draw near to God and He will draw near to you."* So go ahead and take the first step.

For a time, your sin of addiction has separated you from God. But the minute you repent and get back on God's path, the relationship is restored and God is ready to connect.

God never limits the relationship. You do.

Softening a Hardened Heart

Having a hard heart is not unusual for those who perpetually go astray. To soften your heart, you must acknowledge your need for a relationship with God. It's not enough to know who God is, or to understand the law of God, or to comprehend scripture. You can't earn a relationship with God; you have to go after it with all your heart.

This week spend an hour interacting with God. Not a total of an hour, rather one consecutive, solid hour. This requires you to plan ahead and schedule the time. We'll show you how to spend the hour with God, using some concepts we learned from a book called, *The Hour That Changed the World.* The book is out of print, but its content is timeless.

We are grateful that author Steven P. Galvano of SG Publications (www.sgww.org) gave us permission to include our illustrated version of the prayer wheel he featured in his book.

As you can see, the wheel starts with praise and it ends with praise. For most Christians, this is a brand new concept.

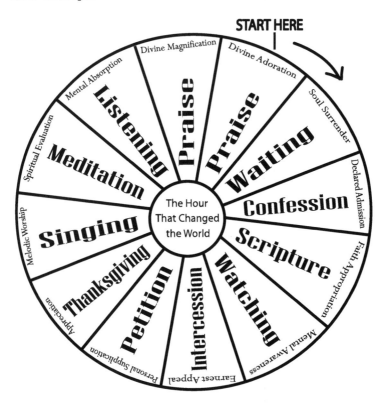

Prayer Wheel

When we give members of a Solid Rock Road group the homework assignment of spending one hour with God using the prayer wheel, the results are always extraordinary. Many people have never spent time interacting with God this way and are surprised to find out they can get inspiration and revelation themselves.

For a lot of people, God is a stranger. This kind of prayer establishes a relationship and turns God into a listener, comforting presence, a father, a friend, and an advisor.

Though God wants you to change, to serve, and to witness to people, the most important thing to Him is having a personal relationship with you. He wants to be thought of, and talked to, and cared about, the same way you do.

With enough practice, you won't need to use the prayer wheel. You will establish a system for entering into the presence of God and hearing His voice. And in the process, you will discover many things about God...and yourself.

The following describes the individual tasks on the prayer wheel. You may spend five minutes or more on each one, but don't skip any of them for the first several times you practice this. If you follow the plan, you will have spent a full hour in prayer.

Praise (Divine Adoration)

Start with praising God for who He is and what He has done. Think about the vastness of God and how He created a perfect universe. You can also thank Him for all the great things He's done for you personally. This is an important five minutes because you are drawing near to God in order for Him to draw near to you.

Waiting (Soul Surrender)

Empty yourself before God and wait for the Holy Spirit to reveal the sins you need to repent of. This removes any barriers to God's presence. In many cases, you may not even be aware of the sin that separates you from God, so be open and willing to identify sin. When you surrender your soul, you are giving up control and are under God's holy microscope.

Confession (Declared Admission)

Verbally confess and repent of any sins you are aware of, and those that the Holy Spirit is revealing to you. This will release you from the strongholds of those sins and open the door to receive guidance from God. When

you surrender your soul and confess your sins, you are
emptying yourself of your sinful nature and letting the
Spirit of God fill you.

Scripture (Faith Appropriation)

Ask God for divine guidance through His Word. Then
open the Bible and read a passage out loud. This may
be a scripture you found prior to your prayer, or you
can allow God to divinely choose your Word for the
day. During this process, we usually pray with the
Bible in our lap, then open it randomly and read. We
then meditate on this particular Word all day long.

Watching (Mental Awareness)

Meditate on the selected scripture and allow the Holy
Spirit to reveal its personal meaning to you. Your goal
is to eliminate all other thoughts from your mind,
except for the Word of God. Read it over as many times
as you need to, then contemplate its significance. You
may think it doesn't apply at first, but wait and you'll
understand its relevance to your life.

Intercession (Earnest Appeal on Behalf of Others)

Intercession is an unselfish prayer spoken for the sake
of other people. Many times we begin this session with
a list of people we have in mind, but then the Holy
Spirit reveals the special needs of others. We believe
this is an important prayer in this process because it is
unselfish and totally service-oriented.

Petition (Personal Supplication)

For many people, petitioning for personal needs comes
first in prayer. But God wants to have your heart and
your mind before He wants to deal with your troubles.
It's true that God answers your personal needs
prayers, but with this process, you're establishing a
relationship first.

Thanksgiving (Appreciation)

This is a chance to let God know you are grateful. Spend time being thankful for what you have, for what God has brought you through, and for anything else that comes to your mind. If you are not grateful by nature, this process will help you learn to appreciate people in your life and blessings you already have.

Singing (Melodic Worship)

Prior to spending your hour in prayer, set up your DVD player, iPod, or other device to play one or more Christian songs that speak to your heart. Whether you have a beautiful voice or a horrible one, stand up and sing your heart out. When you worship with abandon, you are drawing the presence of God to yourself. You will love it!

Meditation (Spiritual Evaluation)

By now, you have opened the windows of heaven and God is with you. Take this time to meditate on the first nine steps you have taken and on God Himself. Allow yourself to absorb His presence and to access the mind of Christ. You may want to picture yourself at the cross of Jesus Christ, and then at the very throne of God.

Listening (Mental Absorption)

At this point, you're able to listen for God. If you wait, He will give you a Word, a mental picture, instructions, or affirmations. Do not leave your hour of prayer without getting God's message to you. Be patient and believe He will speak. If you have to spend a second hour waiting to hear from God, do it! God is always faithful to give you guidance and He will reward your diligence.

Praise (Divine Magnification)

Finalize your prayer by glorifying God as the Almighty Creator of the world. Your hour of prayer starts and ends with praise. And don't cut this process short. After all, you have just spent an hour with your Father in heaven.

Truth at a Glance

There are so many ways to explore truth and to explain the value in studying and meditating on God's Word. That's why there are hundreds of books written on the subject. We believe we've given you food for thought and practical ways to interact with God.

As you walk along The Solid Rock Road and live a clean and sober life, you'll make many new discoveries of your own. Meanwhile, we have captured the essence of this chapter with the following bullet points:

- You have to know the truth in order for you to be set free from the lies.
- The truth is found in the Bible, which is the inspired Word of God.
- Beware of any group or person that declares itself as the "all knowing" voice of God. (The Bible says we only know in part.)
- Check every bit of guidance you get or knowledge you receive against the Bible.
- If people say that Christianity is too narrow and too black and white, agree with them, then live according to God's laws anyway.
- If you don't understand the Bible, keep reading it and you will eventually get it.
- Look for Christian role models whose lives are blessed and who live in victory. Then do what they do.
- If you have been saved, remember you are a new creation. Do not let the devil tell you otherwise.

- Find and memorize scriptures you can use to defeat and deflate the devil. In other words, learn to wield the sword of the Spirit.
- Get help when you need it, but make sure your helpers are in a better place than you are, and that their words and direction line up with the Word of God.
- Use the prayer wheel often. Also, customize the prayer wheel if you don't have a full hour available.

In Summary

By now you have figured out that we are not short on words! And neither is God so He inspired writers throughout time to put His thoughts on paper. The result is the Bible, the most widely read document in the world – the living Word of God.

So we'll leave you with God's Word as stated in James 1:21: *"...receive with meekness the engrafted word, which is able to save your souls." (KJV)*

Principle 4: Forgive Yourself and Others

"For if you forgive men their trespasses, your heavenly
Father will also forgive you. But if you do not forgive
men their trespasses, neither will your Father
forgive your trespasses."
— Matthew 6:14-15

W
e are experts on the subject of forgiveness
because we have had a lot to forgive, and
we've been forgiven for a lot. Honestly, we
have had more than our fair share of life-altering
experiences that required amnesty for ourselves and
others. Some events involved enough drama to merit
their own *Movie of the Week.*

In this chapter, Sherry shares scenes of her life to
serve as examples of forgiveness. Neither of us lives in
the past. We are not victims of our experiences, nor are
we merely survivors. We believe what the Bible says in
Romans 8:37: *"...we are more than conquerors through*
Him who loved us."

The Greek word for 'more than conqueror' is *hupernikao*, which describes someone who is super victorious. Since the above scripture uses the word 'we,' that means *you* are included in the *hupernikao* definition.

If there's a difference between the way we live and the way you live, it may be that we have learned to cling to the Word of God and what it says about us. We've let go of our personal perceptions or the world's definitions of who we are. So many people, especially recovering addicts, struggle with this. That's why Principle 4 is such an important one.

If you've been a Christian for a while, you already know what you're supposed to do in reference to forgiveness, but let's take a look at how you are approaching the subject.

If you know and understand the concept of Biblical forgiveness, that's a good thing, but nothing changes. However, if you commit to putting into action the lessons you've learned, or will learn in this chapter, your life will be dramatically improved.

You can free yourself of negative emotions and the responses that follow if you choose to. If you resist the forgiveness process by holding on to any level of anger, bitterness, resentment, guilt, or shame, you won't experience the fullness of your freedom in Christ or the joy that it brings.

That would be a shame, since the best part of being a Christian is being able to laugh easily and to let go of issues and problems quickly.

Forgiveness brings peace. Don't we all seek peace?

Holding on Can Wear You Out

In The Solid Rock Road groups, we describe a monkey who has discovered a banana inside the hole of a tree. Excited, the monkey sticks his hand into the hole and takes hold of the precious fruit. But when he tries to pull the banana out, he can't because his fist is too big.

Unwilling to leave the banana behind, the monkey sits with his hand in the hole and decides to figure the problem out. The monkey turns his hand sideways, to no avail. He then prays for release, and tries to force his hand out of the hole—all without success.

Ultimately, the monkey gets hurt, tired, hungry, frustrated, isolated, scared, and angry. He also begins to think about how unfair things are and claims to be a victim of his circumstances. The monkey is now anything but happy, and even his monkey friends that stop by to chat no longer enjoy his company. All have suggested he let go of the banana that by now has rotted.

Meanwhile, the monkey feels abandoned by the world. As he watches his friends move about freely, depression hits, bitterness grows, and the banana starts to stink. Still, the monkey refuses to let go.

Once fully liberated, the monkey is elated and begins to swing from tree to tree, enjoying his ability to move about freely in the world.

Finally, when the monkey can no longer stand the stench of the rotten banana and he's so weak he can barely move, he opens his fist and releases the bad fruit.

Once fully liberated, the monkey is elated and begins to swing from tree to tree, enjoying his ability to move about freely in the world. But then the excitement wears off, the monkey settles down, and he perceives that all the other monkeys have better and easier lives. He starts to compare himself with others.

Envious of his fellow monkeys, and angry at himself for wasting time with his hand in the hole, the formerly stuck monkey internalizes his frustration and begins to create conversational tapes in his mind that promote guilt and shame.

The monkey calls himself a loser, a weakling, a fool, and other derogatory words that confirm his stupidity and inability to find happiness or success. Soon, the monkey starts to isolate, building thick walls to hide his insecurities and prevent anyone from entering his solitary world where perceived truths have become the reality of his life.

Feeling alone and without peace of mind, the monkey looks back at the tree with the hole and sees a new banana. At first, he refuses to get near the hole or the banana, but soon, the fruit becomes irresistible. As the monkey drifts toward the tree, the other monkeys intervene and warn of its dangers. But the monkey remembers how good it felt to initially grab the banana and has hope that this time the hole will be big enough for his fist to fit through. So, the monkey sticks his hand into the familiar hole and grabs hold of the sweet fruit.

Peace and comfort overwhelm the monkey. The banana feels so good in his hand, and so he savors the moment and enters into the "I have what I need and I've got control again" mode. But the hole still isn't big enough to remove the banana in his fist, and it doesn't take long for the monkey to feel trapped as he did before. Soon, the monkey experiences a familiar cycle of self-pity and deprivation.

Are You Holding on to Rotten Fruit?

In this story, the banana can represent just about anything you grab hold of and refuse to release. This includes things that appear to complement your life, such as a great-paying job that doesn't satisfy your spirit, or a relationship that relieves your loneliness but is as toxic as arsenic.

You also grab hold of behaviors that are clearly dangerous. For example, you may reach for your drug of choice, an alcoholic beverage, or a sexual experience that gives you instant gratification, but will kill your spirit.

If so, ask God to help you let go. If necessary, go back to the Surrender chapter and complete the exercises. You may even want to follow that up with Principle 2, where you empty yourself of your sinful nature and get filled with the Holy Spirit.

It's possible to forgive one day and be angry the next, or to find yourself filled with old feelings of resentment and bitterness down the road.

Give Up the Grudge

For now, we want you to see the banana as an offense or grudge you are holding on to. Many of you will get an immediate picture of a person and a specific conflict in your life. Others of you may have to dig deeper to realize your hand is stuck in a hole as you hold onto unforgiveness. This is especially true if you have already taken steps to forgive certain people and considered your work finished.

From personal experience, we know it's possible to forgive one day and be angry the next, or to find yourself filled with old feelings of resentment and bitterness down the road.

You might see unforgiveness coming at you in its initial stages, but more often than not, the effects of bitterness and resentment appear subtly and only become noticeable over time. Often, it takes someone else to help you see what's really going on.

If you're like us, anger and resentment creep up. Some people think their bad attitudes and mood swings are normal and acceptable. But if you're moody, you may tend to visit unforgiveness or even linger in it at one level or another. Since many people are not forgiving by nature, they're prone to keep their anger in and later obsess about those who have rubbed them the wrong way, or have hurt or betrayed them.

So the first step in dealing with unforgiveness is to admit you have it. As addiction counselors, we have never met a client in the recovery process who didn't hold a grudge or offense of one kind or another. Therefore, we would find it hard to believe that you are in a pure state of forgiveness right now, even if you claim to be.

> ## You can't pick and choose who to forgive, or how much of an offense you'll let go of, or for how long.

Don't stay trapped in your own clichés. Quit mouthing forgiveness while allowing small seeds of old and new bitterness to take root. And let us assure you, the devil is helping to nurture every negative thought and hurt you've ever had. He's counting on your deep-seated hostility to spring up in season like a well-watered weed in summer.

Unlimited Forgiveness

You can't pick and choose who to forgive, or how much of an offense you'll let go of, or for how long. God doesn't allow you to have any limits on forgiveness. For those who are justice oriented, it doesn't seem fair that guilty people are let off the hook. But as Christians, we are asked to look at forgiveness from God's perspective.

Was it fair that the only begotten Son of God died on a cross so that you could be forgiven for your addictions, your crimes, your bad attitudes, and all the other sinful acts you've ever done or will do?

The blood of Jesus covered every ugly deed you've done and every evil word that has come out of your mouth. When Jesus agreed to die for the sins of the world, He didn't pick and choose who would be on His forgiveness list, nor did He offer partial forgiveness for a select few people He considered worse or better than others. In fact, Jesus died for people who don't even care that He died or who mock the whole concept of Christianity.

Christians are instructed to operate with the mind of Christ. Therefore, you are expected to forgive the way Jesus forgave—without any restrictions and regardless of people's guilt or innocence.

You may find that many people you forgive won't even admit they've hurt you, or minimize your suffering at their hands. Some people don't care if they hurt you, or they think you deserved it. Others will be offended when they find out you carried bitterness or anger towards them.

None of that is your concern. God makes you accountable for your actions, and He deals with others when and how He chooses to.

Vigilante Justice

When you refuse to forgive, you have become a vigilante because you're taking God's moral law into your own hands. The fact that you feel compelled to make someone pay for their actions proves that you don't think God's penal system is sufficient.

Consider the movies that promote vigilantes. If you have watched *Dirty Harry* or *The Terminator*, you most likely rooted for the vigilante characters because they were making up for a corrupt or weakened legal system.

If you love justice, these kinds of movies will satisfy your desire that life be fair. But the problem with vigilante justice in the kingdom of God is that it goes against scripture. The question is, would you rather be right or righteous before God.

If you insist on being right, you will hold people accountable for their actions, and many people will agree that you are justified in doing so. At the same time, this gives God the right to hold you accountable for your wrongs. Matthew 6:14,15 makes this point:

"For if you forgive men their trespasses, your heavenly Father will also forgive you. But if you do not forgive men their trespasses, neither will your Father forgive your trespasses."

How many times have you gone to the cross and received forgiveness? How often do you rely on God's grace and mercy? You probably can't put a number on it. Do you see why you have no right to impart your humanistic version of moral justice?

Forgiveness Results in Freedom

No doubt forgiveness is a process that you must initiate, commit to and continue in. But don't think that forgiveness will allow you to change the past. Instead, it will free you to live in the present.

One summer we had t-shirts made with the inscription, "No Matter How Hard I Try, I Can't Make a Better Yesterday." The back of the t-shirts cited Philippians 3:13: *"...but one thing I do, forgetting those things which are behind and reaching forward to those things which are ahead..."*

Too much time and energy is spent on reliving the past when God says not to. In fact, the scripture uses the words, *"Forgetting those things which are behind."* The best way to forget is to first fully acknowledge the reality of the situation, which can be extremely unpleasant.

We have cried our eyes out for days at a time as we've allowed the Holy Spirit to bring us back to places we didn't want to go. But because we were willing to acknowledge the pain, the Holy Spirit was able to gently guide us out of denial and through the process of deliverance and forgiveness.

If you have the Holy Spirit, you have God at work in you, well able to do what a highly educated doctor of psychology can't do.

The Best Counselor

It's unwise to allow yourself to experience your past without the help of the Holy Spirit. To us, that's the danger in secular counseling. You are constantly asked to talk about your childhood and to relive painful memories. Counselors—as wonderful and caring as they might be—have educational and psychological tools they use to ease your pain, but they don't have a connection to supernatural healing and divine restoration.

If the Bible says that the Holy Spirit is our counselor and comforter, then we should have no problem relying on the third person of the Trinity for help. If you've been saved, the Holy Spirit lives in you, and if you've been baptized in the Holy Spirit, then you have a waterfall of divine inspiration and revelation available to you.

If you have the Holy Spirit, you have God at work in you, well able to do what a highly educated doctor of psychology can't do. For example, a psychologist can help you understand and accept your past, but God can supernaturally free you from childhood traumas and horrific experiences in adulthood. A psychologist can provide prescription medication to alleviate your physical or mental suffering, but God can supernaturally heal you.

A psychologist is paid to devote an hour a week listening to your woes, but God through His Holy Spirit is there all day, every day, and He's willing to take your pain, anguish, and worry from you. First Peter 5:7 gives us permission to give all our problems to God: *"Cast all your anxiety on him because He cares for you." (NIV)*

The Throne of Man

Whenever you depend on your own strength, God can't give you His. When you admit you're weak compared to God, He happily intervenes and everything falls into its proper place. So why do we struggle with letting God be God? If it's been proven that our lives work better when God is in control, why do we persist in doing things our own way?

We have thought a lot about why humans forget that God has the power and love we need to live a great life and walk in forgiveness. We could write out a long list of reasons for Christians going in and out of their faith and submitting to God's principles on and off. However, we believe the main problem is that some people are comfortable on the throne and refuse to get off.

Who is on the Throne?

We have sat on the throne since birth. When you were a baby, the whole world revolved around every need you had. Even if your parents weren't the best, your screams and cries earned their attention.

As you grew older, you may have thrown fits to get your parents to do what you wanted, or sulked, or begged, if that worked better. Later, you used other skills in manipulation to get your way. Even when people didn't comply with your wishes, you took whatever steps were necessary to satisfy your personal desires.

When you are on the throne, you believe the world owes you something. You demand respect you usually don't deserve, and you get angry with anyone who refuses to serve you in the way you expect to be served. This is especially true if someone consistently disappoints you. And unfortunately, God can be the focus of your disappointment.

Have you ever been angry that God hasn't done what you've asked Him to do within a specified time?

Have you questioned God's power because you haven't been a recipient of a recent miracle?

While you sit on the throne calling the shots and questioning God, He can't do a thing for you. He won't bless you when you grab hold of a phony scepter and practice witchcraft. When you're reigning and ruling, you are putting yourself above God, which is exactly what Satan did before he was kicked to earth's curb.

There are obvious signs of having kicked God off the throne, just as there's evidence when He rules and reigns. When God is positioned properly, there's an awesome flow of the Holy Spirit. His love, wisdom, and other attributes are at work in your life. And you practice forgiveness on a daily basis.

It's important that you make it to the cross to forgive and be forgiven, but don't forget to visit the throne where you can enjoy the beautiful and peaceful presence of God.

The throne is a holy place. It's where God's plans and decisions are made. Your daily life and your destiny depend on God sitting on His throne and ruling over you. But when you are on the throne, you become full of yourself, which usually results in anguish, worry, and misery. You become the judge.

It's important that you make it to the cross to forgive and be forgiven, but don't forget to visit the throne where you can enjoy the beautiful and peaceful presence of God. In the Praise and Worship chapter, we explain the value in this and go into some detail about how to immerse yourself in the Spirit.

For now, you can follow the steps we've taken to quit languishing in the "what if" or "why me" victim realm. Remember, for every sixty seconds you spend reliving an unchangeable event, you miss out on a full minute of peace and happiness.

Let Go Quickly

If your hand is stuck in a tree holding a rotten banana—otherwise known as a grudge or offense—you should let go quickly. Get off the throne so God can use His power to change your circumstances and your life. Let God be the judge.

Whatever you do, don't take God's moral law into your own hands. Leave vigilante justice up to Clint Eastwood and Arnold Schwarzenegger.

8 A Life-Altering Weekend

Growing up, there was nothing I enjoyed more than adventure and excitement. I loved taking chances and would jump from high bridges with low water levels and from ragged cliffs that were deemed too dangerous for diving.

About the only thing I feared was wearing the wrong shoes according to my wealthy best friend or having my newly ironed hair frizz in the morning fog. Yes, I actually ironed my hair for the sake of vanity and only wore clothes approved by my friends.

Even in my younger days when I was told I had natural beauty, I suffered from insecurity and had a deep-seated need to please others. Their opinions meant more to me than my own.

When I was eighteen, I fell in love with a guy named Jack. I had just started college, so I still lived at home and was under the authority of my parents. When Jack invited me on a weekend trip, my father wouldn't permit it because he believed it was immoral.

To get my way, I lied to my dad and told him I was going to spend the weekend with one of my girlfriends. He approved of my made-up plans, and so that Friday, I excitedly packed my bags and drove off in my 1963 Ford Fairlane 500. I left Santa Cruz and ended up in Ben Lomond where Jack lived.

Jack was a few years older, so he lived on his own. We were in his living room when we began to argue. It went on for quite a while and in the midst of it, we broke up. I ran out of his house. In an emotional torrent, I sped out of his driveway and drove onto the scenic highway that would lead me home.

The Cabin and the Unforgiven Sinners

I had enough sense to slow down, even though I was crying and desperate to get home to my parents and my sister, Jamee, who was my best friend. But then I ran out of gas. In all the turmoil, I had forgotten that the tank was on empty.

I considered my options for a while and decided against calling my parents. Instead, I started to hitchhike to Santa Cruz. As soon as I stuck out my thumb, a car stopped, but I declined the ride because I didn't feel comfortable. A second car stopped, but I refused the ride for the same reason.

Then a third car pulled over. I studied the driver and the passenger, then quickly jumped into the back seat. As soon as I shut the door, I wondered if I'd made the right choice. But these two men had promised to drive me all the way to my parents' house, which was just outside the city of Santa Cruz, up a long windy road in the country.

Soon, the passenger pulled out a joint and lit it. I wasn't against smoking pot in the early 1970s, so I took a hit. The driver then asked if I would mind if he stopped at his house because he'd forgotten something. I was about to say no, when the car swerved from the main road onto a narrow dirt pathway.

My gut began to ache and my heart started to pound. I refused to take another drag from the joint, because I knew something wasn't right. As we drove, I made mental notes of my surroundings, including every turn the driver made. We were headed uphill, deep into the Santa Cruz Mountains, and I wondered who would live in such a remote place. Finally, we came upon a cabin tucked neatly behind a wall of trees. It was old and extremely run down. By now, fear had gripped me.

Part of me wanted to die right then, but the other part of me wanted desperately to live so I could be with my family once again.

Both men got out of the car, but I sat motionless in the back seat. One of the men opened the door and invited me in. I politely refused, but the driver pulled me by the arm and guided me in. The cabin was cold, and I could sense pure evil, even though I'd never come in contact with such a thing before. Looking back, I would say I had literally entered hell.

Without going into too many details, I will tell you that the cabin was a hideout for a motorcycle gang called "The Unforgiven Sinners." As their hostage, every biker who stopped by had their chance with me, and they all took it. At one point, they had tied me to the bed in one of the rooms, and through the thin walls, I overhead them plan out my murder. Part of me wanted to die right then, but the other part of me wanted desperately to live so I could be with my family once again.

Saturday night, a new face appeared in my room. I knew he'd come to rape me, and like most of the men before him, had brought an audience from the living room. Though I'd kept my eyes shut throughout most of the ordeal, I opened them when this particular man was on top of me. Our eyes connected for an instant, but instead of evil, I saw anguish, and for the first time since I'd entered the cabin, I recognized hope.

Soon after the stranger completed the rape, he left the room. I waited for him to look back and tell me more with his eyes, but he didn't. Then I heard him say his goodbyes to the gang and the front door to the cabin shut. I felt like hope had abandoned me.

More happened that night, but I still can't put all the pieces together. I don't know if I slept at all or if I remained awake the entire night. I do know that there were many Unforgiven Sinners that came in, used me, and left. They came alone and in groups. Some were dirty, some had sores, and all reeked of alcohol. But in the early hours of the morning, the door to the room slowly opened, and there was the rapist whose eyes had met mine.

"Shhh," he whispered. "We're getting out of here."

He wasn't exactly a knight in shining armor, but I believed he was an angel. He pulled me up, put one of my arms over his shoulder, and snuck me out of the cabin. Meanwhile the Unforgiven Sinners lay passed out and sprawled all over the living room. I have no idea what he said or what I said, but when we reached the highway, I got out of the truck and he sped away. I ran down the road until I came upon a phone booth and called Jack.

Jack picked me up and we drove to his brother's house. Inside, the brothers loaded shotguns, with Jack's sister-in-law begging us all to stay put. But Jack, his brother, and I jumped into the truck, and based on my memory, drove directly to the cabin. Once there, the brothers stormed through the front door, ready to impart their own style of vigilante justice. However, there weren't any Unforgiven Sinners in sight. Apparently, someone woke up, discovered I was gone, and they all made their escape.

In the back room lay the bloody evidence of my weekend torment. It made Jack mad, but it made me sick. After taking pictures of the scene, we all ran out of the cabin and headed back to town. Meanwhile, Jack's sister-in-law had called the police, so sirens and lights met us halfway down the mountain.

> But that night, anyone who stepped through the cabin doors was expected to take part in the crimes against me.

American Justice

And there began a two-year ordeal with the American justice system. In the end, the three main rapists were sent to prison. The rapist-turned-rescuer received a lesser sentence for his part in my escape and for turning state's evidence.

My rescuer's name was Ed. During the trial I learned that he was a married man who played guitar in a local band. He had met one of the Unforgiven Sinners a few days before my abduction and rape, and had arrived at the cabin to purchase drugs. But that night, anyone who stepped through the cabin doors was expected to take part in the crimes against me. And Ed made the mistake of opening that door.

The trial became my new torment. One of the rapists had been born into a rich East Coast family that had hired a high-powered attorney to defend him. In those days, victims were allowed to be put on trial, and so that's what happened. They put an old boyfriend of mine on the stand to make sure everyone knew I wasn't a virgin.

The defense twisted the story of my abduction and rape to imply that I had gone to the cabin fully intending to party and have intercourse. They suggested that I loved kinky sex and that the reason I claimed rape was because I was worried that Jack would find out about my secret weekend rendezvous in the woods.

No matter how implausible the defense attorney's story was, I felt every verbal courtroom blow to my psyche. Not only did I feel dirty and disgusting from the rape, but I internalized the attorney's description of me as a whore.

The Past Became the Future

How does an eighteen-year-old reconcile that her rapist was also her rescuer? Well, without God and without proper counsel, she doesn't. Instead, I lived with a skewed perception of myself and of men in general. It seemed appropriate that good and evil existed as one and that even in a man's darkness, light could be found.

Later in life, I spent eight years with a man who mentored me in business but beat me down mentally, and worse, strategically planned my daughter's molestation and rape. And while these were a few of the major events in my life, they combined with many smaller and shorter episodes to confirm that I was stupid, crazy, untamed, and unlovable.

The Depths of Deceit

Though the full story of my daughter's molestation and rape is hers to tell when and if she decides to tell it, I will describe a few of my experiences in relation to it. My goal is to help you better understand the difficulty I've had in forgiving myself and others, but also the importance of it.

When my daughter, Rachelle, was five and my youngest daughter, Casey, was one, I went to live with a man who had promised to love me forever. Though I questioned my decision to be with Dennis from the very beginning—and my entire family was strongly against the relationship—I appreciated the expensive gifts Dennis presented me and trusted his words of assurance, which I desperately needed to hear.

Dennis was going to take care of my kids and me. We would be well fed, well dressed, I would have steady work, a stable roof over my head, and Dennis would help me parent my girls. What more could a lost, confused woman ask for?

Nearly eight years later I learned that Dennis never loved me but had seduced me in order to have Rachelle as his future lover. Though it is almost too painful to write about, it's a reality I deal with.

Can you imagine the humiliation and horror of discovering such a deep level of well-strategized deceit? Can you imagine how it feels to know that I fought for my right to be with a pedophile who intended to rob my little girl of her innocence, and was successful?

When Dennis' evil deeds were exposed, I immediately sought the help of a psychologist and an attorney who were my associates. I counted on them to be voices of justice and logic. But instead, they proved to be friends of Dennis. They were both on his payroll, so every ounce of professional wisdom I received from them was given to protect the man they knew had raped my daughter.

On their advice and with their help, I fled to Mexico to escape the repercussions of Child Protective Services. What I failed to realize was that the actions of CPS were intended for Dennis, not me. CPS wanted to protect the girls and me from further harm, but I was so out of balance, I didn't know what was real, or what was right, or who to trust.

Since it is too long and too involved a story, I will just say that at one point I came to my senses and sought the help of the legal system. Dennis was arrested and charged with crimes against my daughter. However, with the help of the business community in Scotts Valley, California, he posted bail as he awaited trial and continued to live his life and do business as usual.

In court, my family filled the first two rows of seats on the right side of the room. On the left, there was standing room only as people swarmed into court to support Dennis, offer testimonies of his goodness, and to volunteer as his probationary sponsors. Most had sent letters to the judge, declaring Dennis an outstanding citizen and a great friend who had accidentally fallen in love with Rachelle.

My daughter was only twelve when the news of her rape broke out. Dennis was forty-eight at the time, but these citizens were blind to the age difference and the perversity of the acts against Rachelle. They looked the other way when they learned that when my daughter was five years old, Dennis introduced her to pornography, and at age seven began taking sultry photographs, and at the same time, warming her in bed at night for more adult things to come. They ignored the fact that Dennis had a history of child molestation and admitted to having done evil to my daughter.

Over time, and in His time, God revealed the things I needed to see about myself and my experiences.

Reconciling the Past Through the Cross

People have a hard time believing this story because it is so far-fetched, but I have newspaper articles and court records to prove it all took place.

Some people have a hard time understanding how I could have been so manipulated and intimidated by this man, but don't forget, I had suffered from insecurity my whole life. I felt I had to please people whose opinions meant more to me than my own. On top of that, I had internalized the rescuer-rapist mentality and operated from the perspective that light could live amid darkness—that good and evil happily co-existed.

You may think that I have come to terms with all this because I've had years of therapy. But psychology didn't play a role in my recovery. In fact, therapy increased my anxiety and intensified my inner turmoil. Over time, and in His time, God revealed the things I needed to see about myself and my experiences. And once they were exposed, I didn't use my past as an excuse to wallow in self-pity or continually beat myself up for being so confused.

It's true that bad things have happened, but they aren't happening any more. It was all real, but it's no longer my reality because I choose to look ahead, not behind. Some might say I am in denial, but denying the power of God to transform my life is true denial.

I've been through a lot to forgive all those who sinned against my daughter and me. But in every situation of forgiveness, I have had to extend amnesty well beyond the main perpetrator. And God wants you to do the same.

Later, you will be asked to do an exercise that will lead you through the steps of forgiveness. Expect many surprises and revelations as the Holy Spirit guides your personal process.

Forgiving Yourself

Many people find it easier to forgive other people than themselves. Some Christians actually mistake self-imposed judgment for humility. But that's not right. He wants you to be free. If you are a recovering addict, you may have a lot of things you have to forgive yourself for. This can only happen if you admit and acknowledge your mistakes and change the way you behave.

If you are no longer using drugs and have repented, then you should no longer be condemned for those actions. The devil is the one who condemns. God offers opportunities for conviction, which leads to repentance and freedom.

I had a hard time forgiving myself for allowing Dennis into my life and for going against the better judgment of my father and family who warned me about him. In fact, I hated myself for having put my daughters in harm's way. Unfortunately, this self-hatred caused me to deny the pain and resist healing.

When I finally realized that God expected me to forgive myself, I agreed to go through the painful process. With the help of the Holy Spirit, I tore down the walls that protected me for a time. In doing so, God restored our family and we became living examples of how "*the truth will set you free.*"

In the case of the gang rape, I believed I was a fool for running out of gas and an idiot to hitchhike. I was sure the rape was my fault because I chose that specific car to get a ride home, I took a hit from a stranger's joint, and didn't jump out of the car when my gut told me I was in trouble. Also, I didn't fight my rapists, and the list of my crimes against myself went on and on.

The most troubling offense in this situation was that I'd broken my father's heart. I'll never forget his arrival to the hospital following the rape. I had never seen such a level of pain and rage in my life, nor have I since. And though my father shouted out his plans to kill my abductors when he first heard the news, he was instead rendered helpless because I needed his comfort. So there he was, lovingly holding me in his arms and at the same time, having murder in his heart.

At one point, my dad excused himself from my hospital room, and as he walked away, I heard him ask himself, "Why did I let my baby go? Why did I let her go?" And even though I was in a state of shock, I sensed my dad's inner struggle, and of course, I took all his pain and despair on myself.

If we deny our part, we can't forgive it. So, in order to forgive yourself and others you must first acknowledge your role in every situation, then move forward with "forgetting the past" as scripture commands.

I've had to forgive and forgive, then forgive again my rapists, the men in my life, my daughter's molester and his supporters, the overly lenient judges, self-seeking attorneys, twisted psychologists, and many others used by the devil to damage my mind, soul, and spirit.

I dare to think how many times in a day I have had to forgive myself. I haven't always done it willingly, but it's my spiritual duty, so I obey. ■

Forgiveness Defined

Wikipedia defines forgiveness as "The mental and/or spiritual process of ceasing to feel resentment or anger against another person for a perceived offense, difference, or mistake."

It's ironic that the dictionary refers to our offenses as perceived. In other words, your perception of a situation can be totally different from someone else's.

In determining whose perception is right, we're sure the truth lies somewhere in the middle of two differing scenarios. Even if one person has a better point than another, God doesn't care. There isn't a single scripture in the Old or New Testament that suggests you discover who's more at fault or who is more to blame in a given situation.

In Matthew 18:21-22, Peter asked Jesus how many times he was supposed to forgive someone who sinned against him. Jesus' answer must have shocked Peter as much as it surprised us the first time we read it: *"I tell you, not seven times, but up to seventy times seven." (NIV)*

According to our math, that's 490 times we're supposed to forgive one person. After studying these verses in depth, we believe it's 490 times in a single day. God is always so relevant. He knows our hearts are wicked by nature and that we will forgive one minute and become bitter the next.

To end resentment or anger toward another person, we must first agree to do things God's way. In some of the more serious circumstances, forgiveness will require divine intervention. Ask for it!

Just like God knows our hearts, he realizes that some of the more horrific experiences are bigger than our humanity can handle.

Just as God knows our hearts, He also realizes that some of the more horrific experiences are bigger than our humanity can handle. This is why God offers us supernatural assistance.

What Forgiveness Is and Isn't

Forgiveness isn't easy, nor is it an option according to God. But when you do your spiritual duty and forgive, it does make your life a lot better. Think back to the monkey-and-banana scenario. Once the monkey let go, he started to swing from tree to tree. Life was more fun and he was free to be who he was born to be.

We've known a lot of people who refuse to forgive because they think they are required to forget or deny that something bad happened. But forgiveness allows you to remember an incident without having negative reactions. Most importantly, when you turn in your vigilante badge and forgive yourself and others, you're putting God on the throne where He can properly dole out divine justice.

It may appear that someone is not getting what they deserve and justice is not being served, but it is. Just read Revelation 20:12-15 and you'll realize that everyone will stand before the eyes of fire and answer to God.

"And I saw the dead, small and great, standing before God, and books were opened. And another book was opened, which is the Book of Life. And the dead

were judged according to their works, by the things which were written in the books. The sea gave up the dead who were in it, and Death and Hades delivered up the dead who were in them. And they were judged, each one according to his works. Then Death and Hades were cast into the lake of fire. This is the second death. And anyone not found written in the Book of Life was cast into the lake of fire."

God decides the ultimate fate of every human. His final review will send a person to the fiery pit of hell or to the gold-paved streets of heaven.

Though some people will receive leniency while on the earth, no one escapes the final judgment. God decides the ultimate fate of every human. His final review will send a person to the fiery pit of hell or to the gold-paved streets of heaven. There's nowhere in between.

We would like to believe that Dennis, the child rapist, is destined for hell. In fact, we have had a great deal of satisfaction believing this. However, Dennis has the opportunity to get saved and repent for his crimes. If he does, and his heart is right, Dennis will go to heaven. The same is true for the Unforgiven Sinners who were rapists and murderers.

In 2 Peter 3:9, we see that God offers amnesty for everyone: *"The Lord is not slack concerning His promise, as some count slackness, but is longsuffering toward us, not willing that any should perish but that all should come to repentance."*

Why Forgive?

It's impossible to be ruthless and righteous at the same time. Therefore, to be right with God, we must take the high road of forgiveness. It's not always easy, but unfortunately it's always necessary. We're entitled to our initial feelings of anger, but then we have to do what the Bible says.

Unforgiveness blocks our relationship with God and hinders our blessings.

The following are a few key points to remember when working to forgive people:

- Forgiveness is for ourselves and God, not necessarily for the offender.
- We have to keep moving forward.
- We cannot act as vigilantes.
- Vengeance is God's, not ours.
- Our past should only influence our future in the most positive ways.
- When we forgive, we break soul ties to that person and are free to enjoy life.
- God says that forgiveness is our spiritual duty.
- If we don't forgive others, God won't forgive us.
- Unforgiveness keeps us bound up in resentment, anger, bitterness, guilt, and shame.
- Unforgiveness blocks our relationship with God and hinders our blessings.

 Partner with the Holy Spirit to forgive yourself and others. Some of you may want to include your pastor in the process or another Christian known for having a healing and deliverance ministry. Whether you undergo the forgiveness process alone or with someone to support you, we urge you to take this exercise to heart.

Dig deep so you can get rid of any seeds of bitterness or resentment. Leave nothing for the devil to use.

Get your journal or notebook out and write down the following questions. Pray and ask God to help you answer each one and to identify every bit of unforgiveness you carry. Write as your thoughts unfold so you can come to some important conclusions at the end of the exercise.

1. Is there anyone that you have tried to forgive but had a hard time doing so? What holds you back?
2. Is there anyone that you have refused to forgive? If so, what keeps you from it?
3. Whom must you continually forgive? How often are you willing to forgive this person or those people? Once in a while or 490 times in a day?
4. Have you forgiven the people who were not directly involved with an offense but may have played a part in it?
5. What have you held against yourself? What will it take for you to forgive the mistakes you've made?

God's Kind of Love

If you're honest, you will have discovered unresolved issues in all five areas in the above list. Given the opportunity and as long as you're ready, God willingly shows the errors of our ways.

So far you've learned many reasons why it's necessary to forgive, but the final word is that God wants us to love one another, with His kind of love, not our rendition of it.

Ephesians 4:31-32: *"Let all bitterness, wrath, anger, clamor, and evil speaking be put away from you, with all malice. And be kind to one another, tenderhearted, forgiving one another, even as God in Christ forgave you."*

Colossians 3:13 says: *"Make allowance for each other's faults, and forgive anyone who offends you. Remember, the Lord forgave you, so you must forgive others." (NLT)*

There's a difference between thinking you have forgiven yourself and others and actually doing it. Don't justify yourself or defend your need to hold someone accountable. If Jesus can forgive all sinners, you can forgive those who have hurt you.

The Forgiveness Prayer

Below is a forgiveness prayer that will help free you from offenses and grievances. Take the time now to pray and prepare your heart to forgive. Then, say the following prayer aloud:

Dear God:

You sent Your Son Jesus Christ to die on the cross for my salvation so that I can receive forgiveness and offer it to others. I know that in my own strength and in my own flesh, I don't have the ability to forgive the way You do, which is completely and forever.

I realize that unforgiveness stands in the way of my personal relationship with You. Today I am clearing the path by emptying myself of all roots of bitterness, resentment, hurt, and anger.

*First, Lord, I have to forgive myself for [**name the issue you have with yourself**]. Now I will trust Your word that I am forgiven. From this point on, I will not look back at these things, except to use them as a testimony to Your power, authority, love, and grace.*

*Secondly, I have to forgive others. So, in the name of Jesus, I forgive [**name the person or the people**] for [**name the offenses**]. I release everything I've held onto and repent for invoking vigilante justice. I put God back on the throne so He can reign, rule, and judge. In so doing, I repent and release all bitterness, resentment, hurt, and anger.*

Thank You, Lord, for the freedom You bring. I say these things in the name of Jesus Christ. Amen.

In Summary
When you complete the process of forgiveness, you may immediately feel free and want to celebrate. But if you don't feel any different than you did before, don't let Satan lie to you and tell you nothing happened. A lot happens in the spiritual realm that we're not always aware of.

Forgiveness is a lifetime process, so don't get worried if you get bound up again. Instead, repeat the surrender and forgiveness prayers, then let God have the full responsibility for judging mankind.

Principle 5: Be Accountable, Belong and Be Vulnerable

"If we say that we have fellowship with Him, and walk in darkness, we lie and do not practice the truth. But if we walk in the light as He is in the light, we have fellowship with one another, and the blood of Jesus Christ His Son cleanses us from all sin."

— 1 John 1:6-7

In our experience, those with a history of substance abuse often feel rejected by society, churches, friends, and even their families. While it may be true that people have distanced themselves from you, the fact is, you have rejected the values and advice of these individuals and communities, thereby separating yourself from them.

Over the years we have tried to prove that given enough attention and love, the chronically addicted will get sober and become functioning members of the Christian community.

Unfortunately, we have never been able to show positive results from our love-them-enough-and-they'll-straighten-up theory. In many cases, too much compassion has proven to be a huge mistake. We learned the hard way that an overdose of human mercy can actually prevent the love of God from doing its perfect work.

No amount of human kindness can equal God's love. Even so, our humanity often surfaces and we overstep our spiritual bounds. We have offered love in place of God's other hand, which is necessary for discipline and correction.

For many years, we over-practiced our mother's philosophy of "Kill them with kindness." She was right to promote the Christian value of loving your enemies. But like many other mercy-prone people, we managed to take this saying out of context and to the extreme. We weren't just overly kind to our enemies, we were that way with everyone, including those who continued in their addictions well after salvation, and for years into their Christianity.

We have learned to ask God what we're supposed to do when someone is about to relapse or has gone off the path on a mission to destroy lives and break hearts. We have often been surprised by what God would have us do or say in those situations.

Offering kindness in place of truth or correction can interfere with God's process and plan for recovery.

If we were to act on our natural tendencies, we would assault addicts with grace and love scriptures. But in some cases, God has asked us to get a little tougher, to quit offering words of wisdom to the spiritually deaf, and to make addicts completely accountable for their behavior. This often means allowing or promoting serious consequences.

We're not always happy with the directions God gives us because we feel sorry for people who are in darkness, and because we dislike confrontation. But if we don't obey God, or if we soften the blow with a sweeter version of a sour message, then we're in rebellion right along with the addict. The bottom line is that offering kindness in place of truth and correction can interfere with God's process and plan for someone's recovery.

How many times have you taken advantage of a mercy person? Are you always drawn to the Christian who has the most time to spend with you, the most prayer available to you, and the one that is quickest to help find you a place to live and get your life back in order?

We don't blame you for seeking those people out because many are called to the recovery ministry and have special grace for you. But if you've connected with mercy people over and over again, but still aren't free of your addiction, we suggest you find the toughest member of a church and ask them to mentor you this time around.

How God Works

God is love, but He also has all the characteristics of an ideal father. Those who live by the Spirit have both natures as well. In fact, many books have been written about loving the lost and spiritual parenting.

Spiritual parents are responsible for the souls of their spiritual children. That's why God gives them the ability to understand and deal with certain people, along with a father or mother's heart of love. Therefore, the people God has assigned to you have a special anointing for the work.

If God was only love, then the Bible would promote co-dependency, but it doesn't. We could cite scripture after scripture that tells Christian leaders to teach and disciple people, but to warn those in spiritual danger and to pull back from those who aren't putting Biblical instructions into practice.

Other scriptures ask leaders to have patience, and still others say to pray and fast. Even though God uses many methods to get Christians to listen and obey, He doesn't encourage leaders to support never-ending sin cycles. Instead, He asks them to assist in the death of the sinful nature.

> **Anyone who cares about you has made hard decisions based on your actions and behaviors.**

If you are a Christian with a long history of relapse and continued abuse of drugs or alcohol, you can count on God's love, but you can't expect grace and patience forever. Romans 6:1,2 says this: *"What shall we say then? Shall we continue in sin that grace may abound? Certainly not! How shall we who died to sin live any longer in it?"*

We don't doubt that in your addiction you have either been loved to the extreme or felt unloved and abandoned. In either case, you have seen yourself as a victim. But we can assure you that anyone who cares about you has made hard decisions based on your actions and behaviors.

Your loved ones, including your spiritual parents, have probably tried every available method to help you get sober and live a better life. If they are distant from you right now, you should assume they had to get out of God's way and let the chips of your life fall wherever they will.

We're not just addiction counselors with stories about other people to tell; we have family members and friends who are chronically addicted. Therefore, we have personal experience with trying to straighten people out in our own strength.

We have given addicts shelter, counsel, food, money, time, love, and whatever else we thought they needed. And yet, some have consistently returned to their drink or drug of choice and continued making the same mistakes over and over again—for years at a time. Many have come close to death, and several died from an overdose. We've attended funerals that broke our hearts because their children had so much sorrow, and so many questions.

We hate seeing people in captivity, even those who put themselves there and refuse to escape when the keys of freedom are offered. We couldn't be in this kind of ministry if our hearts weren't right. But mercy comes with a price if we allow ourselves to suffer other people's pain and misery more than they do. That's why truth and mercy must kiss in The Solid Rock Road groups.

The Bible says it like this: *"Mercy and truth have met together; Righteousness and peace have kissed."* (Psalm 85:10)

Get and Stay Accountable

When we review our ministry, we see that some Solid Rock Road participants failed to follow through with many of the life-saving, drama-prevention techniques we offered. They listened, understood, and believed what we were saying, but didn't do what we suggested or what God commanded.

We have witnessed this phenomenon so many times, we're about ready to explode. We've often said we feel like the robot on the old TV series "Lost in Space" who flaps his steely arms all over the place and cries out, "Danger, danger, Will Robinson!" only to have the devilish Dr. Smith disconnect the wiring to silence the truth.

Modeling Obedience

Since becoming a Christian, you have most likely disagreed with the advice of your pastor or leader at one time or another. In that case, you did what you thought was right instead. But it's a mistake to ignore counsel from those God puts in your path. Obedience doesn't require agreement; it's an act of self-denial and surrender.

If you agree with someone's advice, then it's not necessary to obey; you are simply following instructions. True obedience happens when you do something you don't want to do.

When Jesus went to the cross, He modeled obedience and surrender. The night before He was to be arrested, Jesus sweat blood in the garden of Gethsemane because He had a negative human reaction to the concept of suffering. He knew what must be done, but He didn't want to take on the sins of the world, or to be temporarily separated from God. Ultimately, Jesus obeyed out of pure selflessness and submission to God.

Romans 5:19 states: *"For as by one man's disobedience many were made sinners, so also by one Man's obedience many will be made righteous."*

This scripture proves two things. First, we are born with Adam's sin nature. More importantly, through Jesus' obedience we are offered a new way of life that empowers us to overcome our sin nature and be right with God. It also requires obedience.

If you remain selfish and stubborn, you'll never achieve righteousness or radical recovery, let alone enjoy your moments of sobriety. When constantly bucking the system of God, you are never happy to be part of it. Instead, you work to control and manipulate God and everyone around you so that you can have things your way.

Having things your way is the reason you're reading this book. Your way obviously doesn't work.

Breaking Bad Spiritual Habits

The more you study the Word of God and the more you pray, the more you'll realize how much you don't know and how much you need strength, instruction, and inspiration from God and others. Those given authority to speak into your life have moral compasses that direct them toward scripture and spiritual responses, thoughts, and answers. God gives them advice and warnings meant specifically for you.

Hebrews 13:17 makes this point: "*Obey your leaders and submit to their authority. They keep watch over you as men who must give an account. Obey them so that their work will be a joy, not a burden, for that would be of no advantage to you.*" *(NIV)*

You would experience radical recovery if you listened and followed detailed advice from those offering wise counsel and spiritual truth. Every time you reject good Christian advice, you miss out on godly opportunities for complete deliverance.

Over the years, we've asked a lot of people who relapse why they didn't do what they were told to do. The following are the four universal answers we've heard:

- "I'm tired of being told what to do."
- "My pastor (or leader) doesn't know everything."
- "The advice didn't seem right to me."
- "They are not God."

No one likes being told what to do, especially if it goes against instinct and logic. But there isn't a single scripture that includes the phrase: "If you think it's right," or "If you feel like it."

There are spiritual implications when you resist or reject counsel from those in authority over you. First Thessalonians 4:7-8 provides insight: "*For God did not call us to uncleanness, but in holiness. Therefore he who rejects this does not reject man, but God, who has also given us His Holy Spirit."*

If a righteous man or woman is teaching you how to live a holy life and everything they teach is backed by scripture, you should listen and obey. When you reject their counsel, the scripture says you're rejecting God.

Christian Nomads

We have known many people who hold grudges against people who have given advice and held certain standards of behavior. Instead of working to attain the standard or adhere to the values, they find fault with whoever gave them the directions, then quickly look elsewhere for help and acceptance.

Christians in recovery are notorious nomads! They bounce from church to church, complaining as they arrive and pointing fingers as they go. They are mad at the pastors who didn't love them enough or feed them spiritually. They are also disappointed in the members who didn't do enough, say enough, or give enough.

Though we have gone beyond the caretaking boundaries our pastor has given us, many addicts have accused us of not caring enough. After they received friendship, fellowship, and discipleship, they wandered away, grumbling about our lack of love and acceptance.

The next thing we know, they have hooked up with another church ministry in town, talking about the same issues they talked to us about. If they are challenged again, they'll move on to the next grace-filled Christian who will listen and help them get back on their feet.

The Sin of Addiction

Addiction is sin and must be treated as such. To get rid of sin you have to suffer all the way to the cross. To remain free, you must assimilate into the Body of Christ. You're supposed to make the world a better place to live. It's not up to the world to make yours better!

Suffering all the way to the cross means you have resisted every physical urge and/or mental temptation to use. But to take it a step further, Jesus, while hanging from the cross and in excruciating pain, actually refused the pain reliever offered to Him. He suffered all the way to death.

The one thing you refuse to do is usually the one thing that God wants most from you.

This is key to your Christian walk. You may suffer to get sober, but if you don't kill your self-will at the cross of Jesus Christ and feel the pain of it, you haven't completed the work.

When obedient, you heed the advice and guidance of those who have been put in authority over you. You don't try and slip under the obedience radar or do nine out of ten things asked of you. You do it all. You complete the process, no matter what.

The one thing you refuse to do is usually the one thing God wants most from you. In fact, you may find out that the whole test of your obedience lies in that one direction given you.

Recently, we were counseling a single mother we'll call Julie. She had relapsed, but sobered up and was having trouble managing her two daughters. We could see she was overwhelmed with life, so we limited our advice to two things.

Our first instruction was for her to recite the Lord's Prayer over her daughters every night before bedtime. She quickly agreed it would be a good idea. The second thing was to get rid of the secular, heavy metal music she listened to in her car and at home.

Julie looked at us like we were crazy, but agreed to it. Unfortunately, Julie wasn't completely obedient.

She listened to less of the music, but refused to get rid of it altogether. She wanted the results, but wouldn't pay the cost.

Today, Julie still listens to secular heavy metal music, and so do her daughters. She has relapsed several times since we had our initial conversation and is currently backslidden and using drugs. Her daughters are teens who are having sex and following in their mother's addiction footsteps.

> ## Christians in constant recovery have to make their church rounds more than once.

The music Julie listens to is dark, but even if we had asked her to get rid of her Barry Manilow CDs, Julie would have been wise to do so. It would have proved she was willing to kill her self-will, be obedient, and quit doing what was right in her own mind.

The town of Medford is small, so Christians in constant recovery have to make their church rounds more than once. Like Julie, many have returned to Joy Christian Fellowship and claimed to be home again. They come to service for a time and appear to get replanted, and then suddenly they disappear again.

These people become homeless by choice, wandering the streets looking for recovery handouts. They're holding up spiritual "Help wanted" signs instead of ones that read, "Will work for sobriety."

God gave his only begotten Son so you could live a good life. Jesus walked Himself to the cross and died for your sins so you could live a good life. The Holy Spirit lives in you so you can access the mind of Christ. The Trinity has done its part, but you have to do yours.

People think God is like a magician because He can do the miraculous. But He isn't into tricks. God holds onto His right to choose when miracles take place and when it's time for Christians to endure a test or take a leap of faith.

God is all-knowing, all-powerful, and everywhere present. If God can create the world with just His words, He can surely change your circumstances ... if He thinks it's best, and if it's the right time.

You may want certain things, but as a Christian you are often asked to give up your personal desires in exchange for God's life plan. And, you are expected to be accountable.

Accountability Defined

Being accountable is more than keeping in touch with others or showing up for church, although these are good first steps. Accountability includes obedience and surrender.

The Wikipedia definition of accountability confirms this point: "Accountability is the willingness to stand up and be counted. In this sense, then, accountability is less something you are held to, or something done to you; rather, it is a word reflecting personal choice and willingness to contribute to an expressed or implied outcome."

Accountability is not an obligation; it's a choice. That's why so many recovering addicts fail in this area. They feel obliged to follow directions, but after a while they get tired of having to account for their words, actions, and behaviors. Instead, they choose to fade away, or decide to change who they are accountable to. But the definition above doesn't give room for this. It says that those who agree to be accountable are willing to contribute to a specific outcome.

The outcome of those in authority over you is complete deliverance from your addictions. If you eliminate or interrupt the process of accountability, you disengage the process of radical recovery.

 Write down the names of people who have ministered to you from the point of your salvation until now. Then write down the advice they've given but you didn't follow. Include the reasons (or excuses) you rejected all or part of their counsel.

Be thoughtful and honest. This is an important step in helping you grasp the concept of accountability. We believe you'll realize that you weren't always willing to suffer through your situation to the point of complete victory or death to self-will. At many crossroads, you became disobedient to your spiritual leaders.

Human Discipleship

Christians are people, and people are flawed. Still, God elected humans to disciple other humans. Even with weaknesses, God set the process of discipleship in motion. He could have chosen to send angels as spiritual guides, or created a super-human species to play the role, but He didn't.

God uses humans to teach and correct other humans in the kingdom of God. In 1 Thessalonians 5:12,13, the Apostle Paul writes, *"Now we ask you, brothers, to respect those who work hard among you, who are over you in the Lord and who admonish you. Hold them in the highest regard in love because of their work."* *(NIV)*

In his book *Under Cover*, John Bevere describes the importance of being submitted and protected by divinely inspired authority. Bevere also warns about the consequences of disobedience, citing 1 Samuel 15:22-23: *"...behold, to obey is better than sacrifice. For rebellion is as the sin of witchcraft...."*

Can Christians actually practice witchcraft? According to the prophet Samuel, we can. We admit to having practiced it ourselves while thinking we were doing well.

We strongly urge you to read *Under Cover*. It's a must-read that will teach you a lot of things you didn't know. The bottom line is, God will NEVER bless you for dishonoring your leaders. Even if your leader is wrong, God honors you for honoring them.

Fight to Belong

If you have been a Christian for a while and still feel more connected to your old lifestyle, you have to turn that around. When you're in the midst of your addictions, you will naturally feel more connected to like-minded people.

In your sin nature, you want to hang around people who are doing what you're doing, or are worse than you. They make you feel better about yourself. No matter how crazy the environment gets, you would rather be with those who don't appear to be judging you or limiting your behavior.

When Satan divides, he conquers. When you give in to your feelings of inadequacy, unworthiness, or insecurities, you're letting the devil win the battle of your mind. If you never get over believing that you don't belong, you will never actually belong.

We're really proud of a friend of ours who constantly battles with insecurities. The way she has fought against the enemy's plan to keep her separated from other church members is to admit when she is feeling unloved, neglected, or judged. When she confesses these things, she brings the dark parts of her mind to the light. This eliminates the power of the lie and allows her to have proper fellowship with Christians and with God.

This friend is an example of how Ephesians 5:8-11 works: *"For you were once darkness, but now you are light in the Lord. Walk as children of light (for the fruit of the Spirit is in all goodness, righteousness, and truth), finding out what is acceptable to the Lord. And have no fellowship with the unfruitful works of darkness, but rather expose them."*

Like many others, our friend will most likely have to continue to counteract the thoughts in her mind. Eventually, her default mode will be who Christ says she is, not what her parents or other people have said about her at one time or another.

Fortunately, our friend has been willing to expose her weaknesses, which has helped keep her drug free for six years. What a great example of how to be accountable and vulnerable. She knows she belongs, even though she doesn't always feel like it, and even when she feels separated and disconnected.

We wish there were more like her in the world. We would be in the midst of a radical recovery revolution!

 When you keep your feelings and experiences to yourself, you can become hard-hearted and insensitive to God.

Allow Yourself to be Vulnerable

The secrets you keep always work against you. And yet, you keep secrets to protect yourself. This is a dilemma everyone faces in the recovery process: Will you be honest and allow people into the deepest, darkest areas of your life?

If you think people won't like you because of what you've done, welcome to the club. We used to believe the same lie. Then we discovered that in our vulnerability, people liked us even more. There is something wonderful about letting the truth be known and being free to be who you are with all your flaws and idiosyncrasies.

When you keep your feelings and experiences to yourself, you can become hard-hearted and insensitive to God and others. When your heart is hard and you protect the darkness within, you lose your compassion and easily become numb to personal sin.

Hard-heartedness even affects your mind. Without true conviction working in your life, you downplay your bad behavior and justify the compromises you continue to make. Without a subdued mind, you filter out God's love and give free reign to your self-will.

If you have a hard heart, you will often confess that you don't feel God's love. In actuality, you're the one holding emotions at bay, including your love towards Him. With an absence of love flowing in and out, your heart gets harder. You then neglect prayer, praise, and worship because you don't feel the need or have the desire to approach the throne of God.

Without connection to the Holy Spirit, you grow colder toward your Christianity and your selfishness grows. We know it seems far-fetched that a lack of vulnerability can cause hard-heartedness, and yet, Christianity is full of such subtleties.

If you've been hurt by people when you've been vulnerable, it's understandable that you would hesitate to open yourself up to others, but it is *not* acceptable. You are going to have to overcome your issues with trust in order to soften your heart.

Satan wants you to be fake and wear a Christian mask. He prefers you to be secretive and deceptive, so do whatever it takes to reveal the truth of your life.

Many Christians walk into church with smiles on their faces and praise on their lips, but go home and suffer in misery. They live with issues that cause them to be depressed and uncomfortable in their own skin. For those with addiction issues, withholding feelings will create a never-ending cycle of relapse. Any way you look at it, secrets are bad for you.

Let yourself feel what you're supposed to feel. Even Jesus displayed emotions because He was fully man and fully God. How awesome is it that God presented Himself through humanity so He could better understand the temptations and wars that rage in our souls.

As a man, Jesus expressed Himself many times in scripture. Jesus felt joy (John 17:13), he had empathy (Matthew 9:36), and had compassion (Matthew 14:14). If you recall the account in Mark 3:5 when Jesus went into the Temple and threw over the tables, then you know He experienced anger. Jesus wept, cried out to God, and sweat blood.

The Bible says we are not to let our feelings direct our thoughts and actions. However, if you hide your feelings, they automatically control you. Also, if you hold back parts of yourself, you will eventually feel like a phony. Therefore, tell someone you trust everything about yourself.

At first, you may not be comfortable sharing thoughts you have always kept secret, but in your vulnerability, you will find freedom. In the process, you may also find a great friend who knows you better than anyone else.

Evaluate Your Relationships

Take a moment to evaluate your current Christian connections. If you're planted in a church, that's good. But you must take a risk by asking someone to be your accountability partner. Let them know you're reading this book and are ready to tell the truth of your life.

If you are a homeless Christian, your first step is to find a church to call home. Once you get planted, ask the pastor if you can be accountable to him, or if he will connect you with someone else who is trustworthy.

If you left a church you were called to attend, then humble yourself, repent, and return. Make an appointment with the pastor and ask him to receive you back. Let him know you are willing to be accountable and vulnerable.

Pastors love to welcome back their prodigals. Just make sure you are a true prodigal—repentant and humbled and ready to stick around.

Are You Part of the Body?

The Bible refers to the Christian church as the Body of Christ, with Jesus as head and members as the body. This is made clear in 1 Corinthians 12:27, which says, *"Now you are the body of Christ, and each one of you is a part of it." (NIV)*

The human body has innumerable working parts, each playing an important role in the body's overall ability to function. When individual parts work well, the entire body is healthy. If one part fails to perform or is missing, the whole body is negatively affected.

Many Christians live as if they are their own entity. In fact, we constantly hear people say they are good with God, have their own relationship, and don't need to go to church to be a Christian.

But that's not Biblical. There isn't a single scripture that promotes isolation or separation. Without attachment to a live body, limbs, organs, and other parts become useless. Ultimately, they die.

As part of the Body of Christ, you have a specific role to play. Later in this book you will read about spiritual gifts, and be encouraged to take a spiritual gifts test so that you can identify your strengths. We give this test in our Solid Rock Road groups and have seen how excited people are to recognize they have special gifts God can use.

If you're a Christian nomad, you aren't connected to the Body. There is a lot written about this concept, but a thorough description appears in 1 Corinthians 12:12-31. We urge you to read this entire passage, but focus on verses 12 through 14: *"The body is a unit, though it is made up of many parts; and though all its parts are many, they form one body. So it is with Christ. For we were all baptized by one Spirit into one body   —*

whether Jews or Greeks, slave or free — and we were all given the one Spirit to drink. Now the body is not made up of one part but of many." (NIV)

People who roam from church to church never feel like they belong anywhere. Picture an artificial limb that functions, but has no flow of the body's blood or DNA. It can connect, but is detachable. It provides a benefit, but is limited.

People who roam from church to church never feel like they belong anywhere.

Connecting to the Body of Christ

People with addiction and relapse issues have a hard time connecting fully to the Body of Christ. There are a hundred reasons this can happen, but there is no viable excuse. You can't let your insecurities, fear of judgment, judgment of others, feelings of unworthiness, or anything else stop you from joining a church family. There is nothing better than to be considered a son or daughter of God, but never underestimate the importance and joy of having brothers and sisters in Christ.

As an artificial limb, you're associated with the Body, but you are disconnected from the DNA. If that is true, you will never share the church vision and you won't have a heart for the pastor or the people.

You may actually prefer being an artificial limb because that allows you to escape accountability. Unfortunately, you can run from God's people but you can't run from God.

The last Principle of The Solid Rock Road is "Serve God and Others." Therefore, it's important you recognize your artificial connection now because you will never feel compelled to serve when disconnected from God and your church's DNA.

To correct this problem, we suggest the following plan of action:

1. Admit you aren't connected.
2. Get planted in a church.
3. Find someone in your church you can trust, then confess that you are an artificial limb.
4. Take the spiritual gifts test described in the next chapter.
5. Attend every church event you can.
6. Invite Christians for dinner. Breaking bread (eating) is a Biblical activity.
7. Continue being transparent. Let another Christian in on your private thoughts.
8. Be accountable to God. Tell Him everything. (He already knows, but He loves to hear it.)

Don't Run from God

Many people think of Jonah and the big fish as more of a fairy tale than an actual account. It seems unlikely that a human would live through the experience of being swallowed by a massive fish who then spit him back on shore. But as we have come to know God and to understand the lengths He'll go to make a point, we believe there really was a man who lived for a short time in the belly of a sea creature.

Jonah was a prophet. One day God instructed him to preach in the city of Nineveh, but Jonah hated the Ninevites. In complete disobedience, Jonah boarded a ship heading the opposite way. Soon, a major storm threatened to sink the ship. Since Jonah was identified as the reason for the problem, he willingly was thrown overboard.

You would think if someone was thrown into a raging sea, they would drown or be eaten by a shark. But instead, a big fish swallowed Jonah alive. Can you imagine how dark and unpleasant it must have been inside a stomach working to digest food? Jonah may have preferred death.

In the midst of the darkness, Jonah cried out to God and repented for his disobedience. In response, God spoke to the fish, who vomited Jonah out onto dry land. Jonah then obeyed the call to prophesy at Nineveh. This one act of obedience turned 120,000 people to God.

Your disobedience may not get you in a whale-like belly at sea, but it will send you to some extremely dark places on land. With your history of drug and alcohol abuse, refusing to do what God wants or what those in authority ask of you can lead you straight to the depths of your addiction. That may be why you're in such a deep pit right now.

Like Jonah, your repentance and willingness to obey can move you toward your destiny. You may not turn 120,000 people to God in one shot, but your legacy will turn the hearts of many for generations to come.

Be Mindful of Your Affiliations

People with similar sin natures tend to find one another, even in church. But it's sometimes better to associate with people who aren't struggling with addictions. You should find friends who have strengths you don't have.

Even if you feel strong in your sobriety, a friendship with a recovering addict who is weak can be troublesome, and in some cases, dangerous. We have seen a lot of people relapse because they thought they could help out a fellow addict.

The typical model for counseling addicts is to provide special weekly meetings where recovered or recovering addicts gather to discuss their specific issues. And yet, the Bible doesn't speak of such meetings.

God is not caught up in the type of sin you have been involved in, He only cares that you take advantage of the cross to get free.

We can't find a single scripture that promotes separation by sin. It doesn't take a recovered addict to free people from the bondage of addiction. The Bible says the power of God frees everyone from whatever sin they are captive of.

Our pastor has a church with many recovering addicts, even though he has never once experimented with drugs or alcohol. With an emphasis on holiness, he preaches the Word of God and deliverance at the cross, and its power transforms lives.

The sin of addiction is no different than fornication or envy. God is not caught up in the type of sin you have been involved in (except the unpardonable sin). He only cares that you take advantage of the cross to get free. He is known for putting people in your path that will lead you there.

Don't be convinced that your job as a Christian is to save the world from addictions. Having been an addict does not qualify you to fight that specific battle. You have to be called by God into the addictions ministry in order for you to be effective. Unfortunately, many former users of drugs and alcohol become artificial limbs in the Body of Christ. They place themselves in recovery and counseling positions when God may want them attached to a different part of the body.

If you feel like a misfit in church, this could be your problem. Maybe you're supposed to minister to children, or be active in the deacon ministry, or serve as an usher or greeter. Perhaps you're an evangelist who should be gathering people downtown on Friday nights.

Only God knows what you're supposed to do, so you have to ask Him for guidance. And don't forget that

God puts dreams in the hearts of children. Perhaps it's time to remember your dreams and to act on them.

You might need to serve in several positions before discovering your true ministry. Our philosophy at The Solid Rock Road is to say "yes" to anyone in church who asks for help, including someone who hands you a toilet brush.

Finding Friends

In recovery, I'm sure you've been asked to say goodbye to unhealthy relationships with certain friends and family members. It was good advice, but we do understand why you hesitate or refuse to separate yourself from people you love and feel comfortable around.

It's even hard to disconnect from people that make you feel miserable. Unfortunately, God is not all that interested in your comfort or emotional attachments. He cares more about your freedom from addictions, your connection to Him, your availability to assimilate into the Body of Christ, and service in the kingdom of God.

If you're expecting radical recovery, then you have to make some real radical decisions about your relationships. We doubt you will have much trouble figuring out who is good for you and who is not. But to confirm what you already know: Don't hang out with anyone who has current substance abuse issues. That includes your best friend, your father, and your mother—Christians and non-Christians alike.

Second Corinthians 6:14 says this: "*Do not be yoked together with unbelievers. For what do righteousness and wickedness have in common? Or what fellowship can light have with darkness?*" (NIV)

This scripture tells you to separate from anyone in darkness. By doing so, you will have a better chance of staying straight. More importantly, you will be creating a path for others to follow along the Solid Rock Road.

Don't be insensitive to people who aren't ready for radical recovery or life transformation. Let them in on your decision to change and give them a preview of what that means in your relationship with them. Some will support you, others won't. Some will want to hear about your journey, so tell them everything God is doing in your life.

For those resistant to God, simply live your life according to Christian principles. They will eventually come to terms with your decision or choose to follow your lead.

There may be some friends and family members who hate your choice to become an uncompromised Christian. Your words may not change their mind, but your prayers and behavior can.

J **Getting Set Apart**
I have visited many prisons and am compelled to watch programs about the prison system. It is a whole other world inside the walls of San Quentin and Pelican Bay, but my perception is that prison is a microcosm of the world at large. The difference is that sin nature is exposed and running rampant.

In prison, the sin nature gets well fed by others who perpetrate evil and accept it as a social norm. And there are many contradictions. For example, convicted pedophiles are detested and targeted for death while dominant male inmates who perform sodomy on weaker young inmates are honored and admired. Yet, both acts are perverted and despicable.

Inmates who are satisfied with their criminal status and have no qualms about acting out their sin nature will usually claim membership with a gang.

Years ago, I wrote a full-length manuscript about an ex-con who had become one of the highest ranking members of the Nuestra Familia (NF). The NF was a

Northern California prison gang unofficially birthed at San Quentin in the late 1960s. Its mission was to oppose control of the Southern California-based Mexican Mafia.

The north declared war on the south in the California penal system. There was so much tension and violence between the gangs, jailors were eventually forced to segregate known members. In the early years, they were separated through solitary confinement. Later, certain prisons began exclusively housing NF members while others held only the Mexican Mafia.

Membership in either gang was for a lifetime. Often, prisoners who associated with members were either tricked into the gang lifestyle or joined voluntarily because they were attracted to the NF's power, protection, and presence.

Inmates who wanted to be free from gangs risked their lives to make such a drastic change. They humbled and surrendered themselves to the incarceration process and began to associate with the like-minded, including members of rival gangs who wanted the same kind of freedom. At the point of assimilation, this group of prisoners started on a journey to discover their purpose. Many received vocational training and even graduated from college while incarcerated. A number of them turned to God and spent time reading the Bible and attending church.

When released from prison, those who removed themselves from familiar prison circles were also able to turn their lives around on the outside. Those who resisted change and maintained their gang affiliations returned to a life of crime and often ended up back in prison.

You may never have been to jail or prison, but in your addiction, you associate with like-minded people and live by the rules and norms of the group. The only way to separate yourself is to surrender your need to congregate with old friends, dysfunctional family members, and others with addiction issues. Then you can connect more fully to the Body of Christ and enter into God's assimilation process. ∎

In Summary
Our Solid Rock Road groups have been profoundly affected by the Accountability Principle. Some say it completely changed their Christian walk. Therefore, we're overwhelmed with the need to get this subject across in the manner it truly deserves. Fortunately, John Bevere has done a great job of discussing kingdom authority in his book *Under Cover*.

Meanwhile, we pray that we have at least shown you the value of connection and assimilation as it relates to your journey towards radical recovery.

Principle 6: Stay Close to God Through Praise and Worship

"Ascribe to the LORD the glory due His name; Worship the LORD in the splendor of His holiness." (NIV)
— Psalm 29:2

When do you give God praise? When your circumstances are good and all is well in your world? When God has answered all your prayers and prospered you? That's when most people appreciate who God is and what He does. That's when most Christians tend to be grateful and thankful.

Don't be ashamed if this is true for you. We've been guilty along with everyone else who talks about how great God is one day, then questions His motives the next. We've wondered if God knew what time it was, and if He understood that the eleventh hour had arrived.

If you're honest with yourself, you will have to admit that at times, it's not only hard to praise and worship God, but nearly impossible to interact with Him.

Everyone has moments where they wonder where God is. Usually, God's asking that about us.

J Consumed with Distress

Recently, I was expecting some money to come in that didn't. Though I was disappointed and on the verge of worry, I figured the best thing I could do for myself and my family was to get happy and not fret about the dwindling bank account. But the financial disappointments continued to pile up, one after the other. When I thought it couldn't get any worse, it did. And every time I figured things were about to get under control, they didn't.

As the pressure mounted, I did what every self-respecting, faith-talking Christian might do under the circumstances; I prayed for the windows of heaven to open and for blessings to pour down. I repented and asked God to show me any areas of sin in my life, and to show me where I'd gone wrong in the area of stewardship.

I agreed with God that testing my family was good and would further develop perseverance and trust. And of course, I rebuked the devilish devourer who was stealing my blessings and joy.

The bank account battle went on for many months, and with it, a battle in my mind. I would go as far to say my thoughts were nearly consumed with my distress and the questions I had about why nothing worked in my favor when I was doing everything right.

But as all moments of truth do, it finally came to me. I had done everything a self-respecting Christian would do, but hadn't done what a true lover of God does. In the midst of my worries and selfishness, I neglected the most important relationship in my life. Sure, I had been praying to God, but I wasn't spending time with Him. I hadn't visited the throne room of God, the place where I would find His presence and the peace I so desperately needed.

When my mind was filled with the frightening reality that I might not be able to pay bills, the promises of God got buried under the anxiety and fear. Of course, I didn't wake up one morning in fear for my finances. The process was more subtle than that, slowly building to a point where I nearly forgot that God is my provider and He will save the day! Even the memories of past miracles and blessings faded into the dark recesses of my mind.

Meanwhile, the Giant of Lack reared its ugly head and made a lot of noise in my head. I kept hearing, "See, the blessings weren't real. There's a good reason for you to worry about your money. You are not God's favorite. Everyone else is being blessed, but why aren't you? There's something wrong with you. God isn't going to save the day this time. Your luck has run out."

With these kinds of thoughts filtering through my mind, I couldn't help but doubt God. And yet, I still managed to talk a good faith talk. I told everyone who would listen that I trusted God, when in reality, my confidence had waned. I figured that my role as a faithful Christian depended on the words that came from my mouth, which is only partially true. I understand now that what God required of me during this struggle was a steadfast spirit and a true demonstration of faith.

It's not hard to cite faith scriptures, or even to teach on the subject of faith. However, to demonstrate faith in the midst of a major life crisis can be one of the most difficult things a Christian is asked to do.

What I've discovered is that such a deep level of trust can only be gained through an intimate, daily encounter with God and the consistent appreciation for who God is and how He works. ∎

Praising in Times of Trouble
In Psalm 112:6-8, David helps us understand what it means to have confidence in God: *"...a righteous man*

will be remembered forever. He will have no fear of
bad news; his heart is steadfast, trusting in the LORD.
His heart is secure, he will have no fear; in the end he
will look in triumph on his foes." (NIV)

This scripture tells us that it's not only important to
have faith in the midst of a disaster, but we have to be
careful about how we see the future. Do you have a
sense of impending doom or one of impending blessing?
If you can't see victory ahead, you have an unsteady
and insecure heart, and it's easy to believe you often
choose to use drugs and alcohol.

> God wants us to rely on Him for all our answers
> and solutions. God wants us to experience His
> comfort as we endure life's experiences.

During a recent Bible study, we asked a group of
women if they feared bad news or ever worried about
problems that didn't yet exist. Every one nodded their
heads yes. One young woman said she constantly
worried about her husband and children, even when
everyone in her family enjoyed health and happiness.
We then asked the group how they responded when
legitimate bad news came their way.

We weren't surprised when the woman began
talking about how fast she became entangled in
negativity and fear, and how she perceived that new
problems proved she was right to worry in advance.

To see how genders differed in this area, we talked
with a group of men about the concept of fear and
learned that the mere thought of bad news required
them to immediately solve a problem. Since the
problem was non-existent, it was impossible for them
to figure out what to do. Therefore, men who are prone
to fear have a tendency to feel incompetent and
frustrated at the same time.

Both genders fear potential problems and the onset of bad news. The difference is that women get ready to fix the people involved while men are more inclined to want to fix the actual problem. Either way, this is counterproductive to Christianity since God wants us to rely on Him for all our answers and solutions. God wants us to experience His comfort as we endure life's experiences.

If you attain something easily, it isn't necessary to have faith for it. In your earliest Christian days, God blessed you without your even trying. Do you remember when everything seemed to go your way without much effort? You knew it was God then.

If you're like us and most other Christians in the world, you find it hard to believe that God is involved when your needs and desires are put on hold. It seems like God doesn't care when you pray for relief from financial stress, or are fighting the urge to use drugs or alcohol. Yet, the opposite is true.

It's because God cares that He allows you to suffer longer than you think you can. Read the book of James. It begins with a discussion on perseverance and patience. He wants to teach us to understand the difference between our ways and His ways. For those who consistently self-medicate and interrupt the process God has them in, God's ways don't make sense at all. And they never work because addicts never complete the process. They never endure to the end. They lose faith.

According to Merriam-Webster's Dictionary, faith is "An unquestioning belief that does not require proof or evidence." If that's the accepted definition of the word, then you have no right to ask God to prove He is answering your prayers. Instead, you have to live your life knowing that He is. This is nearly impossible unless you worship God at His throne and learn how to praise through your problems. When you visit the throne, you realize that God is God and you are not.

A Cry for Help

There is a time and place for crying out to God in your distress. In fact, it's Biblical to yell, "Help!" But you can't spend your entire Christian life as a chronic crier. If you read the book of Psalms, you'll see that David wasn't afraid to tell God his feelings. David consistently thanked God for coming to his rescue and saving him – well before it had actually happened.

David had intimacy with his Creator and was a perfect example of pure trust in God. The reason David could praise and worship God in the midst of being tested was because his love and trust for God overpowered his fears and sin nature.

If you want to love God like David did, you will have to enter a deeper dimension of prayer, praise, and worship. Only then can you make the great exchange from fear to faith.

It's possible to have a sense of impending blessing in the midst of a disaster. You just have to remember that God's intended end for you is always good, even when things look bad. And, you will have life-changing prophetic revelation in times of need, rather than fear the future as it appears to be unfolding.

At this point in your Christianity, love must replace your logic. You must believe that two plus two doesn't always equal four. With God things don't have to always add up, they can multiply. If God wants, He can subtract or square things off. If God is God, He can stretch your income beyond mathematical laws. God can choose to give you back more than you allowed the devil to take, and He can give you blessings well beyond your highest expectations.

This is good news if you choose to change. Some of you have created deep wells of debt and even wound up without homes, cars, and other possessions. Many of you have lost your children, or your spouse gave up and left. If everything is lost and everything is broken, then God may have you right where He wants you.

A Matter of the Heart

We used to wonder why God wants the adoration of humans, especially since He knows our hearts. According to Jeremiah 17:9, *"The heart is deceitful above all things, and desperately wicked..."* But it's His way of connecting, and God knows that His presence can soften our hearts and remove evil from them.

The Bible says that David was a man after God's own heart. If you have ever been after someone's heart, you know what it takes to get it. You think about that person day and night. You're consumed with what they think and remember the words they speak. You are kind and loving to that person and want to spend time with them more than you want anything else. When you have hope that love will result, you will do whatever makes that person happy and you will make sure that you touch their heart.

David deliberately put God first. He kept his heart pure and devoted to God. That doesn't mean David never made mistakes; we know he did. The Bible tells the story of David's lust for Bathsheba, the sins that followed, and the consequences of his poor choices.

You desperately need the heart of David. And you need to get your truth from the inside out.

Still, David didn't let his past mistakes keep him from connecting with God. In fact, he was more devoted afterward and more inclined to visit the throne because he knew how much he'd grieved God, and better understood the mercy of God.

Psalm 51:1-6 provides insight into how David's sin and suffering allowed him to fully experience God's redeeming love. We used scriptures from The Message because it totally reveals David's heart.

"Generous in love – God, give grace! Huge in mercy – wipe out my bad record. Scrub away my guilt, soak out my sins in your laundry. I know how bad I've been; my sins are staring me down. You're the one I've violated, and you've seen it all, seen the full extent of my evil. You have all the facts before you; whatever you decide about me is fair. I've been out of step with You for a long time, in the wrong since before I was born. What you're after is truth from the inside out. Enter me, then; conceive a new, true life."

At this point, David didn't blame anyone else for his mistakes. He wasn't rationalizing or justifying his behavior. Instead, he acknowledged his evil and gave God the right to change him. That's why in Acts 13:22, the Apostle Paul refers to David as a man after God's own heart.

You desperately need the heart of David. And you need to get to your truth from the inside out. Therefore, we suggest you read the entire book of Psalms out loud, day after day. No matter what other scriptures you read, add Psalms to your devotions.

Before you recite David's words, pray God will exchange your hard heart for a God-loving, faithful heart like David's. Ezekiel 36:26 makes you such a promise. *"I will give you a new heart and put a new spirit within you; I will take the heart of stone out of your flesh and give you a heart of flesh."*

Learning How to Praise and Worship

Praise and worship is a lifestyle, not a warm-up session for a Sunday morning sermon.

When you learn to praise and worship in your times of need or in the midst of a crisis, you will discover that it really is possible to have peace when there's trouble brewing and negativity surrounding you. It's possible to be content even though you don't have what you want, or even what you think you need. Simply put, your peace and happiness don't depend on what you get, but who you get to spend time with.

Your problems don't stop you from getting into God's presence. Obsessing about them, and trying to solve them on your own, are what hold you back and make you miserable.

If all you ever do is ask for things, you have the wrong concept of who God is. He is not Santa Claus!

Misery has a mind of its own if you let it persist. Wikipedia describes misery as "a feeling of great unhappiness, suffering and/or pain." Your addiction promotes your misery, and vice versa. It's a vicious cycle, but it's what you've come to know and accept in your life.

At times, our misery increased our worry and heightened our fear, which all worked to further distance us from God. On certain days, we admit to not having a prayer in us. We not only failed to get to the cross where we could release our burdens, we didn't even get close to the throne where God fellowships with us. In retrospect, we see our times of prayerlessness as some of our darkest days.

What about you? Are you going to love God when He isn't giving you what you want when you want it? Are you a fair weather God lover?

When we experience miracles through God and read about the blessings and promises in store for us as Christians, we can get over-focused on the gifts. We should be grateful and remember God, but we can't act like spoiled brats expecting more and more without giving anything back. When you are after someone's heart, you have to give your heart to that person. The same is true for God.

If you have been disillusioned with Christianity or stumbled in your walk with God, it may be that you have had a one-way relationship. Actually, there is no such thing as a one-way relationship because it takes two ends to connect to even have a relationship. You expect God to connect with you, but have you made any effort to connect with Him?

If you pray, you are accessing God, but you are not necessarily enjoying a relationship with Him. If all you ever do is ask for things, you have the wrong concept of who God is. He is not Santa Claus!

What you have to remember about problems is that their levels of seriousness are relative, and everyone has them. If you were to discuss tests and trials with your pastors, elders, leaders, and fellow church members, you would discover that everyone is either in a test of faith, or just coming out of one. The difference in their stories is that while some have lost their confidence in God, others are living out Hebrews 11:1 and taking ownership of the scripture's promise. *"Now faith is being sure of what we hope for and certain of what we do not see." (NIV)*

Those who get to the throne of God through praise and worship learn how to own the scripture and reap the benefits of His presence and peace in their situation. They aren't necessarily having fun or enjoying the process, but they are growing with God. They are moving to deeper spiritual levels, which is the reason God allows tests to arise and continue.

Without intimacy with God, you won't understand Christianity, you'll only be subject to its laws. What a drag that is.

When you learn how to praise and worship, the following are some of your rewards:

- You will be in the presence of God.
- As a believer, you are empowered.
- Your anointing will increase.

- The gifts of the Spirit are enacted.
- You will remember past miracles and future promises.
- God will re-establish your focus and vision.
- You will have rest and peace.
- You defeat the devil and his evil spirits

The Magic of Music

It's no secret that we are without musical talent of any kind. We've never been happy about it, but we have learned to be content with the fact that God didn't gift us with beautiful voices or the inclination to play an instrument.

Yet, when it comes to listening and loving music, we have a lot of experience. In the old Santa Cruz days, we would find a band we liked and follow them to all their venues. We were good for these bands because our enthusiasm for their music was contagious. As groupies, we pulled in the audience with our clapping and movement.

In a secular sort of way, we were praising and worshipping. We were connecting with the members of the band and making sure everyone else enjoyed them as much as we were.

When we became Christians, we changed the music we listened to. If you're in love with secular music and bands of your past, this may be a difficult choice you may have to make. If you're like other people who are learning how to be Christians, it may take time to make this kind of a switch, but we pray that you begin to accept the fact that your music may be counterproductive to your spiritual growth.

As you learned earlier, there is a single path that leads from *salvation* to sanctification, which is where the true blessings of God are found. Your worship through music plays a major role in whether you stay on the path or not.

Since Satan was once the worship leader in heaven, he has used music to subtly destroy God's people. We could go on a long tirade, but we won't. Instead, we'll trust that you will allow the Holy Spirit to convict you if you're listening to music that is not meant for your Christian ears.

In Summary

If you were in one of our Solid Rock Road groups, you would have joined us in an hour of praise and worship as we practiced this Principle together in our living room. You would have been with us as we approached the throne and entered into God's presence and peace. We assure you, there is nothing quite as glorious as spending uninterrupted time with God.

In the otherwise hectic and chaotic lives of people, The Solid Rock Road facilitators provide group participants with rare opportunities to be still before the Lord. For many in our groups, it's the first time they have had a true encounter with God outside of church. We often invite our pastor friend named Paul to lead us into worship. He is a true lover of God's presence.

Paul does a great job of describing the purpose of praising and worshipping, but admits he can't teach people how to love God. If you don't spend time with God, you'll never know Him and you surely won't love Him as deeply as those who get in His presence and stay there.

Whatever you do, never underestimate the value and importance of interacting with God. You can't get too much God. And who doesn't need a touch from the Almighty?

Chasing the High

With your drug of choice, you can use more than normal and still never get the high you want. It's safe to say that you're chasing the high, but can never grab hold of it. No matter how hard you try, you don't get the sense of well-being you're searching for, and you can't really escape the pain or erase the memories of your past. You also have the added burden of being a Christian, which can really ruin a good high. You're so conflicted, it's hard to believe you would subject yourself to such torment..

Even after you have quit your addictions, many of you have tried to ease your anxiety and depression with prescription medications. Filling your emptiness with legal pills is not the cure. Instead, it sends you along the Yellow Brick Road where smoke and mirrors fog up the critical issues of your heart. Plus, you never take your medication as prescribed. You take too much, then have to figure out how to get more – a vicious cycle.

When you approach the throne and wait on God, you will have revelation, inspiration, and motivation. You will fill your emptiness with the Spirit of God and find the peace you need.

 Make a date with God. Plan an hour to praise and worship. As you enter into His presence, visualize the cross and allow the blood of Jesus to cleanse you and purify your mind. As you get to the throne room, we believe you will experience God in ways you have never experienced Him before. Only God can show you the fullness of His love. It's not something you read about it, or hear about. A relationship with God, and a love for God, is something that is caught, not taught.

Relationship (Not Religion)
Relationships can take time, so continue to schedule dates with God and find as many moments to praise and worship Him as you can. God is waiting and

wanting to interact with you on a regular basis. He wants to be in a relationship with you so He can bless you, direct you, and fill that God-shaped vacuum in your heart with His love and essence.

In Proverbs 8:17, He says, "*I love those who love me, and those who seek me diligently will find me.*"

Principle 7: Seek the Will of God for Your Life

"For I know the plans I have for you," says the Lord. "They are plans for good and not for disaster, to give you a future and a hope." (NLT)
— Jeremiah 29:11

If you have ever wondered what in the world you're doing on this planet, consider yourself lucky. Just asking "Why am I here?" is proof that you have at least begun your spiritual journey towards your true purpose. If you have been a Christian for a while but haven't figured out that there's more to getting saved than accessing the grace of God, it's time you dig deeper.

You should be desperate to discover your destiny, not desperate for your next high. What keeps you sinking to the depths of your addiction is either your ignorance about God's will for your life or your refusal to comply.

When you seek the will of God for your life, you are re-attaching yourself to the original plan God set into motion before you were born. If you're not excited or even slightly motivated by this idea, you probably haven't taken the steps in this book seriously. Don't be discouraged if you need to go back and revisit one or more of the Principles.

Also, your persistent sin of addiction has buried your spiritual life for so long, it may take you some time to get it back. If you want it, you can have it.

Some of you have grown up in dysfunctional families. Therefore, it may be hard to believe that God gave you a special anointing from the beginning or that you would ever be empowered or enabled enough to enact it. But the Bible verse at the beginning of this chapter (Jeremiah 29:11) is one of many scriptures that prove your life is anything but random.

If you grew up in a church that promoted religion and legalism in place of a personal relationship with God, then you may have a warped view related to the gifts of the Spirit. When we were young, we thought that going to church was a waste of time. Neither of us saw the benefit. We didn't realize that church was supposed to be a holy time where we could praise and worship with the Body of Christ, experience the presence of God, and receive the Word as seed for our souls. Plus, we had no idea that God had given us spiritual gifts.

But once we knew this to be true, we set out to discover who we were in Christ and to fulfill our purpose. Along the way, we've discovered that the pew is where the process of perfection begins. It is a sacred seat in the house of God.

Taking Action

Knowing that God has something good planned for your future, and making sure those plans happen, are two different things. You can win a vacation to the

Bahamas, but you have to make arrangements to go, and then you have to board the plane and land there to actually take advantage of the gift.

If you have never been spiritually fulfilled, then I suspect you have never taken hold of the whole portion God has set aside for you. You may have made plans to do so, but have yet to follow through completely. Like the Bahamas and its tropical delights, you hear about how beautiful the kingdom of God is and you want to enjoy it, but you abort the flight that will get you there. As a result, you never get to taste the fruit of the land.

When the devil feeds you, he first seduces you, then fills you with lies, and eventually starves you to spiritual death.

Failed attempts at finding your purpose leave you hungry and thirsty. Your emptiness will have you looking for satisfaction of one kind or another, and of course, in all the wrong places. Very quickly, Satan is there to hand out morsels of the world like candy on Halloween night. If you take what's easily offered, it will please you for a time, but in the end, you crave more but are satisfied less and less.

When the devil feeds you, he first seduces you, then fills you with lies, and eventually starves you to spiritual death. You are blind to the process because it all starts so subtly and innocently. But once things start going downhill, your life is like a runaway train that has so much momentum it can't be stopped. As you well know, the result is always disastrous.

When you sit at the table of the Lord and eat of His goodness, your soul is satisfied and you are inclined to identify and use the gifts God has given you. When you are spiritually gratified by living out God's purpose, you lose your appetite for sin. In John 4:34, Jesus makes this point: *"My nourishment comes from doing the will of God, who sent me, and from finishing His work." (NLT)*

Well-nourished Christians are healthy and active in their ministry. Those who pursue their purpose get properly nourished when they agree in spirit to fulfill their destiny in God. If your spiritual health has deteriorated, or if you have been deficient from the beginning of your salvation to now, you need a spiritual cleansing that will purify your body, spirit, and soul. And, you must immediately re-attach yourself to God's plan for your life.

Obviously, the plans you have made for yourself have made you sick and tired.

Boredom is a Lie

If you're like us and most addicts we know, you're used to living on the edge and become easily bored with anything that resembles a routine, including the process of recovery and your spiritual journey.

We don't doubt that you've been sincere every time you've made a vow of sobriety and a re-commitment to God. But then restlessness sets in and the lies of the devil get louder and more frequent.

If you find yourself asking "What's next?" or "Is that all there is?" then the battle for your mind has already started. The devil thrives on your dissatisfaction and boredom. He will play mind games with you and start telling you that the way to enjoy yourself is to get high.

We recently had a talk with a chronic alcoholic who we'll call Mike. He told us that he had finally identified the specific lie that provided him with an excuse to relapse.

In the midst of his sobriety and just when his life seemed to be in order, he would hear these words from the devil: "It's time to drink. Don't worry. Everything's calm right now so it's the perfect opportunity. You've always gotten out of every mess you've been in. You can do it again and it will be all right. You can fix it later."

The problem with this lie was that there was just enough truth in it for Mike to buy it. He had survived a lot of hell and bounced back time after time. He knows God had mercy on him and that his family loved him and would always end up forgiving him. Mike knew that if he wasted his money on foolishness, he would be broke for a time, but would work hard and make it up.

But then Mike started to notice that each time he relapsed, it took him longer to bounce back and it became harder to get his life in order. His job and relationships were in serious jeopardy and his debt continued to climb. Several times Mike nearly lost his vehicle to the title loan companies who charged outlandish interest rates like the good loan sharks that they are. He was physically ill with Hepatitis C, but worse than that, he found himself on a spiritual death bed, pleading with God for his life.

The devil's plan is to ensure you participate in despicable behavior, then mark you with guilt so you don't dare believe that your divinely inspired dreams will come true.

Most lies of the devil have a realm of truth in them, which is why people fall into deception so easily. It's as if the devil is a merchandising master who places despicable things in beautiful packages and paints pretty pictures of death and destruction. He goes to a lot of trouble to package the lies so we will remember the message. Like all good marketing experts, his goal is to get you to buy into the lie over and over again. If you catch on to his tricks, he'll simply redesign the package to pique your interest once again.

The devil's plan is to ensure that you participate in despicable behavior, then mark you with guilt so you don't dare believe that your divinely inspired dreams will come true. The devil is all too aware that godly gifts are used against him so he will do whatever is necessary to prevent you from identifying them or perfecting them.

Don't feel bad if you have fallen for Satan's tricks. You are not alone. But it's time that you learn how to quickly differentiate between the devil's plans, God's plans, and the plans you make to gratify your own desires.

You need to be clear about who is doing what so you can learn how to consistently make the right choices. Wrong choices result in foolish behavior along the Yellow Brick Road. Right choices set you straight on the path that will satisfy your spirit and bring true fulfillment.

If you were to come to a fork in the road and one sign read "The way to Death," and the other sign read, "The way to Life," which one would you choose? It seems obvious that any sane person would choose The Way to Life. However, if The Way to Death appears to be filled with excitement and fulfillment of lusts, the more popular choice for the chronically addicted is to choose to die.

If you're thinking that you wouldn't be that careless, don't forget that every time you drink or do drugs you have chosen the way to death. You don't have to go on a binge to enact the devil's plan, you just have to open the door a crack. The simplest of compromises can destroy your dreams and kill your spirit.

The next chapter describes in detail the path set out by God. It also provides insight into the plans of the devil, which will prevent you from discovering your special anointing and gifts from God.

Receive the Right Gifts

You don't have control over the spiritual gifts God assigns you, so your goal is to embrace whatever God has blessed you with and do the most with it. The worst thing you can do is decide which gift you want and try and take hold of it. You can practice and practice perfecting it, but the gift will never have the anointing attached to it or the power of God behind it. You may even get frustrated with your pastor or leaders because they don't recognize or use these specific gifts, but they may have better discernment than you. Or, the timing may not be right.

Your gifts are yours alone, and only you can use them the way God intended. Gifts from God are not just special little talents for you to show off to your Christian friends. They are actually spiritual weapons of warfare necessary to protect, defend, and build up the Body of Christ. If you refuse to discover your Godly gifts, decide you don't like them, won't practice the right one, or underestimate their value, you are like a selfish, unarmed soldier who won't take his post and only cares about his personal peace and comfort.

God wants to give us the deepest desires of our hearts. But we must get happy with His timing and His choices.

Whenever we talk about spiritual gifts, we ask people to picture presents under the Christmas tree. Each one has a name attached to it because every gift has been purchased with a specific person in mind. You're not supposed to open someone else's presents, but sometimes we compare presents and wish we could exchange ours for someone else's.

Growing up, Sherry always wondered what everybody else was getting for Christmas. She was envious even before the family opened presents. In fact, our family has old movie films that prove this to be true. There she is, ignoring her unopened presents and watching intently as the rest of the kids opened theirs. She was so pre-occupied with what they were getting that her own presents became less important.

Once in a while our parents would buy the two of us the same gift in different colors. One year we got bathrobes and Sherry wanted Jamee's color. Jamee felt bad so she traded. Then Sherry put it on, only to discover it was too small. Still, Sherry was determined to have the robe so she wore it for a few days until she could no longer stand the discomfort. Jamee agreed to trade back and when she put on the original robe it fit and felt good. Sherry also grew to favor the color chosen for her.

God gives gifts according to His original will for us, and often, according to our prayers. He doesn't always give us exactly what we want, and He sets necessary limits, but God wants to give us the deep desires of our hearts. But we must get happy with His timing and His choices. We must learn to love the color of our spiritual robes.

The Anointing

When God plans to use someone for a special purpose, He imparts an anointing. Throughout the Bible, the power of God was applied directly to humans, and that still happens today. The anointing changes the way a person acts and behaves in the world. Without it, humans are limited.

Some people believe that unless the power of God is demonstrated in a believer, they are not true Christians. In fact, the word 'Christ' actually means anointed. So a follower of Christ, and someone who has Christ living in them through the Holy Spirit, should have the anointing power.

Just because you have acted out your sin nature through addictive behaviors, you have not been stripped of your gift. Instead, it lies dormant until you decide to receive the gift and use it for good. And don't worry, the anointing comes in the fullness of God's timing. He knows better than you when that is.

Discover Your Gifts

There are many responses from Christians in relation to spiritual gifts. Some people always want what someone else has. Others want to discover and use their gifts the minute they are saved. Others appear less interested in the whole concept of spiritual gifts and we would even go as far to say that they are fearful of finding out what God has gifted them with. Finally, there are Christians who just don't care.

You know which category you fit into. For those of you who are anxious to know what God has planned from the beginning, you'll love the test that's included in this chapter. If you're fearful or apathetic, you may not be as enthusiastic, but we urge you to spend the time necessary to complete the spiritual gifts test.

In this chapter, we're giving you a glimpse into the sea of gifting information. The Bible is your best resource, but in addition, there are hundreds of books written about spiritual gifts and you would be wise to study the subject in depth.

We highly recommend you read *Finding Your Spiritual Gifts* by C. Peter Wagner and then take the test that's included in the book. It includes 137 questions and has an easy-to-follow format. Go to www.gospellight.com.

You'll soon learn what your strengths and weaknesses are. You may be surprised. Then again, the test may simply provide the confirmation you need.

Once you make the discovery, bathe yourself in the knowledge of it, pray for the anointing necessary to use it, and ask your leaders to help you grow in it. And please make sure that you look up all the verses associated with your particular gifts.

In Summary

All gifts from God are good. And though they are part of your original DNA, enacting your gifts comes with a cost. Like an instrument, a voice, or a trade, practice makes perfect. So we encourage you to use the results of this test to lead you in the right direction. Then, pay the price for it.

Whatever you score highest in, study the subject in depth. Take what you learn to heart, but don't let your scores box you in. In fact, you may want to work on some of those areas in which you scored low.

In the next chapter, you'll learn the importance of staying on the path that God has led you to. Trust that God has given you the right gift and that He will help you understand and use it for the right reasons. I love what David wrote in Psalm 32:8: *"The Lord says, 'I will guide you along the best pathway for your life. I will advise you and watch over you.'" (NLT)*

If God is guiding you, advising you, and watching over you, then you'll never be lost again.

Principle 8: Stay on the Path God Leads You To

"A man who strays from the path of understanding comes to rest in the company of the dead." (NIV)
— Proverbs 21:16

We're always amazed when addicts find the right path and start living an honorable and blessed life, then suddenly change directions. This is one of our biggest irritations with our recovery ministry. People discover what works, they get sober and safe along The Solid Rock Road, but an off-ramp catches their attention and away they go.

We've asked many relapsed Christians why they went off course. Some said it was because they were bored. Others reported that they were fearful of taking the next step. There's a whole group of relapsed people who claimed that being a Christian was more work than they thought.

Admittedly, the devil has installed plenty of detours that take Christians off of God's well-beaten and blessed path. You may have chosen to take one because it was familiar and seemed like the easiest and fastest way to get you somewhere. Even though your Christian leaders, friends, and family begged you to keep moving forward, you did what comes natural, which is to follow your addiction cycle and the devil's strategic plan for your life.

As you wander from safety, you justify your actions with clever excuses and bold-faced lies. You also get validated from people who either don't understand your addiction or have a secular philosophy.

Veering off the path seems innocent enough, like taking a Sunday afternoon car ride down a one-lane country road. But it's far from innocent. Where the devil tempts you to go isn't where God wants to take you. You know it in your soul, but your drug dealer is waiting and the liquor store is around the corner. Before you know it, there's no turning back.

It's hard to admit you're guilty of cooperating with the dark side of your soul. You'd rather believe you have a chronic disease, and that there's a whole group like you who can't help it.

That might be true for those who don't know Christ and don't understand the power of God or the work of the Holy Spirit. But you do. No matter how well you argue your case, the Bible wins the debate. It says you are more than a conqueror.

To make matters more clear, the Apostle Paul writes in 1 Corinthians 10:13, "*No temptation has overtaken you except such as is common to man; but God is faithful, who will not allow you to be tempted beyond what you are able, but with the temptation will also make the way of escape, that you may be able to bear it.*"

When we read this scripture, we wonder why it's even necessary to write this book. The inspired Word of God says you can escape your temptation. There shouldn't be an argument, but there is because you prefer the secular concept that gives you an excuse for your rebellion.

Here's the real end to the argument: *"Because he himself suffered when he was tempted, he is able to help those who are being tempted."*

Beware of Imposters

Don't get mad at people assigned by God to warn you or redirect your steps. Know that whoever is with you on your spiritual path has been put there for a reason. But don't get confused. Satan wants to plant one or more imposters in your life who will cause distractions, confirm the lies in your mind, and help set your course for destruction along the Yellow Brick Road.

Imposters say they want the best for you, but consistently encourage you to compromise your Christian beliefs. They will not like it when you choose church over a Super Bowl Sunday party, or a Bible study in place of a recovery meeting. They question your level of Christianity and call you over-zealous when you go for God one-hundred percent. They assure you that you are not under the Law of Moses, but under God's grace, which means you are free from adhering to stiff rules and absolute moral truths.

The work of an imposter often results in your doubting what you thought you were sure of.

Imposters have a way of appearing wise when they are fools. They seem kind of right when they are totally wrong and are great at selling you on watered-down versions of Christianity.

Sadly, these imposters show up in church as your friends. You can recognize them because they tend to gossip, talk negatively about the pastor, and complain about the way things are done or how situations are handled. After every sermon, they enjoy critiquing the pastor and pointing out spiritual flaws.

Most people who get you off track don't attend church regularly or aren't even Christians. Imposters have their own spin on God and are driven to share their religious opinions with you. The work of an imposter often results in your doubting what you thought you were sure of.

Matthew 7:16-20 talks about imposters at a higher level, referring to them as false prophets. But we believe we can use these scriptures to define regular people who stand in God's way by offering misguided counsel.

"You will know them by their fruits. Do men gather grapes from thorn bushes or figs from thistles? Even so, every good tree bears good fruit, but a bad tree bears bad fruit. A good tree cannot bear bad fruit, nor can a bad tree bear good fruit. Every tree that does not bear good fruit is cut down and thrown into the fire. Therefore, by their fruits you will know them."

This scripture helps unmask imposters. Just look at their fruit and you will know them. In other words, look at their life and their ministry. Are they serving God and doing His will, or are they doing their own thing? Are they prideful or do they model humility? Are they at odds with the pastor, elders, or other church leaders and members? How are their children doing spiritually?

If a good tree cannot bear bad fruit, then those on God's path will have a trail of goodness behind them and are surrounded with blessings.

One word of caution: Be careful of anyone who claims to be a Christian but refuses to associate with a church. Separation from the Body of Christ is dangerous and deadly. The path of God attaches you to the Body.

The Bible says we all fall short of the glory of God. No one is perfect and we're not asking you to stand in judgment of your Christian brothers and sisters. But have sense enough to know who will be good for your Christian walk and who will cause you to stumble.

For example, if you're prone to depression and negativity, you shouldn't become best friends with someone who is melancholy. If you are an alcoholic, it's foolish to associate with a Christian who drinks wine or other alcoholic beverages in front of you.

Just as people believe they have the right to drink alcohol, you have the right to remove yourself from a situation that is detrimental to your well-being. A good friend or a Christian leader should realize that drinking wine in your presence is stupid.

While traveling along our paths, we have distanced ourselves from certain people we enjoyed being around. It's not easy, but in each situation, it was best. While we're open to relationships with those just getting on the path or those struggling to stay on, we keep a safe distance from seasoned Christians who have become set in their disobedience and who exhibit a vagabond spirit.

While some refuse to attend church, many others go from church to church, looking for the newest mystical experience and resisting God's attempts to get them rooted and planted in the house of His choice. So choose your church friends carefully. It's smart to establish yourself with those moving along the path of righteousness towards sanctification. Their deep roots will help you stay put.

Those with shallow roots or a complete lack of a root system cannot produce good fruit. Whatever you do, don't allow yourself to become someone else's bad fruit.

Tumbleweeds

Christians without roots are like tumbleweeds. They are brittle and blow wherever the wind takes them. Tumbleweeds have been separated from their roots, which are their source of life and energy. Without roots, tumbleweeds become dry, stiff, and easily broken. And, they often get caught up, cornered, and stuck until another strong wind blows it away at random.

Tumbleweeds never follow a straight path. They have no idea where they're going, or will end up.

Tumbleweeds are considered an invasive species, driven by the wind as a light, rolling mass that scatters large numbers of seeds far and wide. As they tumble around, they compete with rooted plants for space and tend to contaminate whatever is in their path. Tumbleweeds are also referred to as noxious weeds, which are harmful to humans.

If you are a lone Christian on a detour, you need to get back on track immediately.

Many scriptures discuss the importance of growing up as strong Christians with deep roots. Study these scriptures and you'll remember that your behavior and character affects everyone in your sphere of influence.

Mark 9:42 says it this way: *"But whoever causes one of these little ones who believe in Me to stumble, it would be better for him if a millstone were hung around his neck, and he were thrown into the sea."*

Throughout this book we warn you about the danger of Satan, but we always bring out the mirror. So look in it. What do you see?

Are you connected to God, your source of life and energy, or are you separated from God and your church family? If you are a lone Christian on a detour, you need to get back on track immediately.

To us, the devil is craftier than he is scary. Most people are on alert for his evil ways when they need to be on the look-out for his clever tactics.

Detours of Loved Ones

The same people who prayed for your sobriety and encouraged you in your Christianity can present detours. This is not a trick or plan of theirs. They just don't understand the danger or the spiritual battle that has been waged against the people of God.

Let's say you have been off of drugs and alcohol for a few months. With the help of God and a support team, you have pulled yourself together. You have been at church two times a week and attended every Christian event on the calendar. You have met with your pastor and asked for help from the leaders. You made new Christian friends and started to read the Bible and pray every morning. Your life and spirit are beginning to soar and you have found peace of mind.

Then you find a job that requires you to work on Sundays. Your leaders and Christian friends tell you to refuse the job because it interferes with church. However, your spouse, parents, and others who have an interest in your life insist you take the position, saying God gave you the job and He'll understand.

Hoping to make up for your mistakes and wanting to put money in your pocket and food on the table, you take the job that requires your Sundays. Within a week you quit waking up early to read your Bible. Before long, you pray only when it is convenient, and you're too tired to make it to church on Wednesdays. Then you start making excuses to miss Bible study.

To your family and others, you're doing great because you are sober and bringing home a paycheck. Meanwhile, you're disconnecting from God and the people who are your life-line. Your spirit gets choked underneath the pressures of your life and the peace of God leaves you.

At this point, you know the job has become a detour, but you have wandered so far from the path you can't even find God on your days off. Eventually, your sin nature gets restored and your negative cycle comes full circle.

Suddenly, the issues of your life resurface and the anger, bitterness, and resentment creep back into your heart and mind. People around you start to notice the negative changes and start encouraging you (or nagging you) to get back to church or to attend ninety meetings in ninety days again.

By now you have become unhappy because you are abstaining from your drug of choice without the peace of God or the benefits of the Holy Spirit. Now, something as seemingly harmless as a job that requires you to work Sundays has set the stage for a major relapse.

If you can't relate to the job scenario, perhaps you'll understand if we discuss the concept of straying from the path for a relationship. Many of you have quit going to church after meeting someone who had less of an interest in God than you did.

You may have thought that God sent you a soul mate when in actuality the devil was playing cupid on your behalf. If you're single and prone to loneliness, Satan will undoubtedly send the wrong person your way. This is especially true when you're experiencing victory over your addictions and are walking with confidence along The Solid Rock Road.

Whenever a relationship takes precedence over God, you have wandered way off track. Therefore, commit to waiting for God to send your true soul mate. If God created the universe, He can surely figure out a way for you to meet the man or woman He has for you.

If you're already in a relationship, you may have to take a risk for the sake of your spiritual health. Stay on the path no matter what your significant other says. You may feel like you're losing your relationship, but one of two things will happen if you choose to stay connected to God and your church. One is that the person will follow you and share your joy. The other is that the person will not. Either way, God will bless your decision to stay on the path.

When you trust God in these kinds of situations, you move forward along The Solid Rock Road.

 Before reading further, let's assess where you stand right now. Pray and ask the Holy Spirit to show you areas of compromise and detours you have taken, and those currently set up for you. Then answer the following questions in detail. Write down what God is showing you. It is important to keep a written record because the devil can trick us into denying what we know.

1. Are you a tumbleweed?
2. Are you willing to stay connected with God no matter what people say?
3. What is your priority? If it's not God, will you do what it takes to seek Him first?
4. Are there any imposters in your life? If so, how will you separate yourself from them?
5. Have you allowed your loved ones to unwittingly interfere with your Christian walk on The Solid Rock Road? If so, how will you help them understand what you need to do?
6. Have roots of bitterness, or resentment re-surfaced? If so, will you re-read Principle 4 and forgive again?
7. Who at church are you being accountable to? (You learned the importance of this in Principle 5.) If you don't have anyone helping to teach and train you, are you willing to search for this kind of support?

God as Your Priority

Matthew 6:33 says this: *"But seek first the kingdom of God and His righteousness, and all these things shall be added to you."* If you would live by this scripture, your life would be amazing.

If you consistently make God your priority, you will have no trouble making good decisions and staying on the right path. But you have to fight for your Christian rights. Sometimes this means you will frustrate or disappoint those you love as you walk the straight path.

Joining the Christian Culture

One battle you face along The Solid Rock Road is finding a way to assimilate into the Christian culture. It's not enough to attend church, read the Bible, and pray. You have to learn how to think and act in a Christ-like way, and you must interact with people you would not normally interact with.

It's common for you and other recovering addicts to gather as a group. While this may be a comfort and a benefit in some ways, there must come a point in your Christianity when you disconnect with your sin nature and start relating with those who don't share your propensity to drink or do drugs.

In recovery circles, people who don't have addictions are often referred to as 'normies.' But let's get real. There is no such thing as a normie. What is normal to some is not to others and everyone is born with a sin nature that brings about issues of life. In God's eyes, we are all fighting the same battle, which is to divert the devil and overcome personal challenges, whatever they are.

Of course, disconnecting from your addictions is the opposite of what is taught in secular recovery circles where group association is preached. But in Christian churches, you don't see all the liars purposefully gathering as a group in church, or all the gossips, all the whiners, all the gluttons, all the hypocrites, or all the proud.

Now, it's true that people with similar sin natures tend to find each other, but that is attraction, not purposeful gathering. And as Christian counselors, we can assure you that individuals who share a sin nature are not always the best for one another.

Two recovering whiners who hang out together will often complain themselves right out of the church. Two rebels will do what rebels do, which is to oppose authority and promote anarchy. And recovering addicts—God bless us all—will most likely set themselves apart. When they do, they limit their learning and feed into the lie that once an addict, always an addict.

It is important for recovered addicts to see that people who appear to have a good life can have problems and circumstances that are sometimes worse than their own.

As you have learned, The Solid Rock Road groups are 10 weeks long. For nearly three months, small groups gather to learn and experience one Principle at a time. Throughout the experience, facilitators encourage participants to assimilate into the Christian culture by attending a weekly Bible study, joining a ministry, serving in the church, or doing something for God outside of themselves.

In the last week, participants graduate with a Certificate of Achievement. This is usually a bittersweet moment because the groups have shared their hearts and bonded.

Still, we don't hold weekly post-recovery Solid Rock Road meetings. If we did, then we would be promoting separation by sin as a practice and a lifetime connection to addiction. These work opposite of Christian theology.

Instead, we guide our graduates to weekly Bible studies where people of all backgrounds gather. It is important for recovered addicts to see that people who appear to live a good life can have problems and circumstances that are sometimes worse than their own. It's exciting when polar opposites discover similarities, celebrate their differences, and learn acceptance.

If you're concerned about other people judging you, then stop judging them.

We love it when the wealthy associate with the poor, and when the depressed interact with the carefree. There is power in this kind of uncommon connection. For example, a parent whose child has died from a disease has different issues than someone who has lost a child (or children) to the foster care system. And yet, the two can relate to each others' emptiness and sadness. The common denominator is that both have suffered a great loss.

If you're concerned about other people judging you, then stop judging them. Many times those who hit bottom look at successful business people as snobs. They could be really stuck-up people, but how would you know unless you interacted with them? At the same time, someone who is down and out may appear to be uneducated and unethical. Then again, they could be brilliant scholars and have come from highly moral families.

Everyone has something to teach and something to learn. Don't miss out on such a powerful dynamic. Don't be hindered by your own separation philosophy or the devil's desire for you to remain separated from the Body of Christ.

Wandering from the Path

Many new believers say they feel like strangers in a foreign land or a fish out of water when they walk into church. While it only takes a moment to get saved, it may take more time to feel connected to the Christian community, and to understand the whole point of redemption and how to live life as an uncompromised Christian.

God wants to know you will stay on the path even when you're bored and when the going gets tough.

Many times, addicts are looking for a quick fix and an instant high, much like the rush they get when snorting a line of cocaine, taking a hit off a crack pipe, or popping pills. You may have expected to be high on God all the time, and were disappointed when the initial excitement wore off. But God doesn't have any interest in satisfying your desperate need for euphoria.

God wants to know you will stay on the path even when you're bored and when the going gets tough. Your habit is to persevere when church seems to benefit you, but then quit when God or His people aren't spoiling you.

For you to get free of your addictions the final time, you must be convinced that going the way of God is the only way to go. You need to make your mind up that no matter what obstacles get in your way, you will continue moving forward on the right path.

To help you understand the insanity of your cycle, we've created the following scenario:

Persevering on the Path

Let's say you applied for a well-paying, permanent job in Thailand and your boss chooses you for the position. However, the job requires that you move overseas immediately. The news is rather surprising, but you are excited and call everyone you know to tell them the good news.

You begin to visualize your new life and see that the doors of opportunity have opened. That night, you celebrate and start looking forward to the changes. You're thankful because you were unhappy and unfulfilled in your current position.

As the excitement wears off, you realize all the work there is to do and become overwhelmed. You have to figure what to take and what to leave behind. You have to pack your entire household, clean your home, get your bills in order, and the list goes on and on. You also realize that once in Thailand, you will have to learn the language, the traditions of the people, and how to get from point A to point B.

Though you're in turmoil, turning the job down is not an option. You know it's the right move so you make up your mind to take whatever steps are necessary to get you to Thailand. Then, as your to-do list multiplies and you are just about to lose your sanity, there's a knock at your door. It's a surprise helper who takes your list and immediately simplifies the process.

"One thing at a time," the helper says. "Let me take these burdens from you." So the helper takes the list and step by step, directs every task, one at a time.

This is how God is when you commit to assimilation, surrender to His plans, and agree to stay on the path no matter what. He will handle the details if you stay put and cooperate with Him. At the same time, Satan will throw your Christian to-do list in front of your face, making you anxious and overwhelmed.

God will help you decipher what to hold onto and what to give away. He will help you clean your spiritual house and provide finances if you allow Him to open the doors of opportunity. God will help you learn His language expressed through the Bible. And you can count on God to put people in your path that will help teach you how to get from where you are now to where you're destined to go.

Just as you would be willing to assimilate into the Asian culture if sent to work in Thailand, be willing to assimilate into the Christian culture.

Fellowship and Guidance

If you need help figuring things out, find a church that has the heart to teach, train, and coach you in your Christianity. These kinds of churches do exist, although many American churches fall short in this area; they allow people to flounder about and try to figure things out for themselves.

This fend-for-yourself technique works for some people who are internally motivated to know God and discover their purpose for living. They have no problem studying the Bible on their own and doing whatever it takes to stay on the path.

But not everyone is like that. We believe God gave us the 10 Principles of The Solid Rock Road to guide those who need it. Many will take our advice and follow the path of righteousness described in the Bible. But if you don't follow the directions, or put Biblical principles into action, you'll never get where you really want to go. You won't assimilate into the Christian culture either, and you'll always feel like a fish out of water.

Well-seasoned Christians know this, but some choose to do their own thing, believing the grace of God will cover them forever.

For now, we want you to get an overall visual of the path that God sets Christians on. We also want to make sure you understand the path that the devil has led you along while in your addiction.

The comparison below is taken directly from the book of Proverbs, which is full of wisdom for every area of life. And as you will see, it provides all the benefits to staying on the right path, and gives plenty of warnings about what happens when you take a detour along The Yellow Brick Road.

Path of God: Solid Rock Road	Yellow Brick Road
God directs you along it	It is deep darkness
It is level	You are in danger
You enjoy peace	You are in the company of the dead
You can run along it and never fall	People rejoice in the perverseness of evil there
It's the way to victory	People along it are devious; they stay awake all night thinking of ways to make you stumble
You travel easy; it is like a highway	You will stumble, but you don't know why
Wisdom and knowledge are pleasant along this path	You are trapped
Your steps are firm	Evil seductresses are all along it waiting to trap you
You will not stumble	Your sin ensnares you there
It is so bright, it gleams	Your sin will be discovered
You get understanding of what is right and fair	You will die for your lack of discipline
You receive everlasting life	Your stupidity will kill you
You will receive a good inheritance	You will die because you are not corrected
It is the way to heaven	You will receive stern discipline
You are safe. God is always watching over it	You will become a sluggard
You will have integrity	It is full of thorns
You will walk with confidence and security	It is the way to your grave
You are protected from wickedness	You will be evil there
The devil can't walk on it	You entice others into sin

8 Saved by Grace

It's not easy staying on the right path, especially if you're not even sure what it looks like. When I was first saved, I didn't know about supernatural power and access to the mind of Christ. Therefore, I let my pot-smoking mind guide my steps. I had been saved for less than a month when all hell broke loose.

I had just learned my live-in boyfriend of eight years had molested my daughter and I feared Child Protective Services would take my children from me. Using fear as a motivator, my so-called friends convinced me that I should flee to Mexico with my two daughters.

What I didn't realize was that the friends helping me escape were actually protecting my boyfriend. They had his best interest in mind, not mine or my children's.

Nevertheless, I gassed up a formerly abandoned 1952 pickup truck that had been gifted to me for the road trip, and off I went. All I had was money in my pocket (the pay-off), a map without a final destination, and sheer terror driving me out of town.

I have a book full of Mexico stories to tell, but in short, God sent angels with me as I traveled south with my girls. When the brakes failed on the old truck while going downhill, God performed a miracle and we lived. When we landed in Guadalajara after a month on the road, God connected us with Christian missionaries who became our friends and family. They helped this frightened and disheartened mother and her two blonde-haired, blue-eyed children find a home, learn the language, and assimilate into the culture.

We spent two wonderful years in Mexico, completely under the grace of God. We had His favor and He made it obvious. But shortly after moving back to the states, I felt a shift. Something different was happening. When God no longer spoiled me, I became frustrated and didn't understand that He was expecting me to take a walk of faith. Instead of going deeper in God, I went astray.

You have undergone the same process, and probably have great memories of God as your protector and provider in the earliest days of your Christianity. But then it seemed that God vanished, and you wondered where He went.

If so, then you reached the same place I did, which is that God had been faithful and was asking us to be faithful back. When we refused, He graciously allowed us to drift.

I don't know how far you've drifted, or for how long, but most addicts tend to get way out there—far, far away!

> I didn't forget all the life-saving miracles God had performed. I just kept hoping He would ride in on a white horse and save me from myself.

I refused to take steps forward in my walk with God and instead began abusing His grace. I falsely believed that God would continue to bless and protect me, even though I quit going to church and kept my salvation a secret.

I returned to my pot-smoking, vodka-drinking life and entered into a series of regretful and miserable short-and long-term relationships. In a way, I was proud of myself for not snorting cocaine or doing any of the hard drugs I was once prone to do.

I didn't forget about the life-saving miracles God had performed for two years. I just kept hoping He would ride in on a white horse and save me from myself. I thought, "If God can work everything out in Mexico, He can do it in America."

But since I quit attending church, there wasn't anyone teaching me the ways of God, or informing me that God could no longer honor my bad choices. I didn't understand that my separation from God was my own fault because I chose to travel along a dark and scary path.

I refer to those days as my personal journey along the Yellow Brick Road. I wandered from job to job, man to man, and even city to city. For a time, I drove a taxi. In between fares, I would park in Jamee's driveway, smoking a joint with her husband Jerry – my favorite pot-smoking buddy – and listening to the radio that would announce my next pick-up.

I later traded in the taxi for a limo. I always drank the alcohol meant for the customer's pleasure. Meanwhile, I lived in ghetto apartments and at one point, moved to a slightly seedy place called the Hitching Post, one of Santa Cruz's infamous down-in-the-dumps motels. (No offense to the Hitching Post. It served a purpose.)

Feeling trapped by my life, I moved from Santa Cruz to Sacramento in 1992. Two years later, I moved from Sacramento to Southern Oregon. I loved this new little town called Talent because it only had one stop light. Though I arrived with the wrong man, it turned out to be the right move.

It took a few years, but I eventually said goodbye to the ungodly relationship and started to pursue God like I had in Mexico.

I started back on the path alone, but along the way, my two daughters and three grandchildren have followed. As I stayed on the path, God sent my soul mate, Alan. We love God and support each other in the ministries and giftings we have been given.

Alan doesn't have the grace for this recovery ministry. Though he is a former addict who went through The Solid Rock Road group, and was trained as a facilitator, he quickly learned he was not called to the ministry.

During Alan's first experience as an intern, he wanted to wring the neck of the participants—the very first day of group. This was not a good sign. We lovingly banned him from leading all future groups.

We are still telling the intern story and laughing with Alan about it. At the same time, my wonderful husband promotes the work and supports The Solid Rock Road team. Meanwhile, he is doing the work of God through the Veteran's Administration.

We all learned a good lesson: God has a path for each of us. We have to find our place and trust God to move us towards our personal destiny. ■

J Staying on the Path--Barely

My husband and I followed Sherry to Talent, Oregon, a town of about three-thousand people, located twenty-plus miles north of the California border. I had been Christian-curious before leaving Santa Cruz, so my goal when I got to Oregon was to go attend church with Sherry. The first Sunday, I responded to an altar call. One month later I sobered up.

Jerry wasn't pleased about my sobriety or my salvation. He'd lost his drinking partner and church interfered with our Sundays. My pastor told me to pray for Jerry, and I did. He came to church with me a few times but was bored and decided that organized religion wasn't for him.

Jerry continued drinking and I hated it. My attitude stunk because he wasn't changing. Jerry was unhappy because I was changing. He wanted the Jamee he'd married, not the sober Christian in the making.

Our unhappiness continued for three years, until neither of us could stand another minute of the tension. Jerry moved back to Santa Cruz and I went on with my life. I remained sober and started to attend Joy Christian Fellowship, although I was still quite a piece of work! Looking back, I see that I needed Jesus way more than I thought I did!

Thank goodness God gives grace and allows baby steps in the first stages of a conversion because that's what I was taking. But baby steps are better than a standstill or a u-turn.

Meanwhile, we started divorce proceedings. While the paperwork declared we had "irreconcilable differences," the real reason our ten-year marriage ended was because I was on a spiritual path that Jerry had no intention of taking.

By clinging to God the best way I knew how at the time, I received His protection and provision.

I knew that getting sober and going for God was a risk, but the preacher kept telling me to have faith and trust God to put my life back together, so that's what I did. By clinging to God the best way I knew how at the time, I received His protection and provision. Today, I rejoice in the good choices I made during the early days of my Christianity, and have forgiven myself for all the dumb things I did. Thankfully, God allows mistakes and shortcomings as we search for truth. And He continues working on our hearts when He sees that we're on the right path.

After seven months of separation and right before the final divorce papers were signed, Jerry had a middle-of-the-night wrestling match with either an angel or God. He was drinking heavily and smoking a lot of pot in those days, but was miserable and wondering if death was next. He wasn't suicidal, he just felt like the end was near.

One night, he woke up from a sound sleep to hear a voice that said, "You are going to quit drinking, go home to your family, and go to church." Jerry argued aloud. "No, I don't want to do any of those things." But the voice persisted and the argument went on and on. Finally, after becoming exhausted, Jerry's response changed. "Ok, I'll do it."

Jerry fell instantly asleep and woke up a new man. He remembers opening the door of his house and seeing a beautiful, bright world. He was delivered from darkness into light, and has never had a drink of alcohol or used drugs since.

Jerry arrived home two weeks later. It wasn't easy for me to welcome him because all the resentment and bitterness was still there. Neither of us was in love with the other, but both of us were being faithful to God. I remember crying out to God and asking Him why He waited so long to answer my prayers. I soon realized that God is the master of timing, and my prayers over the next three days changed. "You were faithful to me," I said, "so I will be faithful to you."

Jerry got saved that first Sunday and the church celebrated with us. Still, we were fighting our feelings of frustration, and bitterness was eating away at us. Our pastor knew of this battle going on in our hearts, but he urged us to trust God, so we did.

Several days later, Jerry started to pass me in the kitchen. I looked at him, and he looked back to me. We found ourselves in an embrace, and within moments every bit of anger and resentment was gone. It's hard to describe, but the best way to explain what happened is to say it was like Cupid sending his arrow through us. We were instantly in love and everything was new. We'd been delivered simultaneously.

We know the Holy Spirit performed supernatural surgery on our hearts. We experienced a miracle that is hard to describe in human terms. And since then, we've enjoyed many other restorative miracles as the two of us walk boldly along The Solid Rock Road.

Miracles and deliverance are amazing, but every Christian can undo what God has done if we stray from the path.

As new believers and under God's saving grace, we can walk imperfectly on the path and still be blessed. But as we describe the concepts of justification by faith and sanctification along the path in the following pages, you'll see that God's grace must be used wisely. You have to believe that the grace of God enables you to resist temptation, not that His grace gives you free reign to live in sin and be forgiven over and over.

Jerry is an ex-junkie with a wild and crazy past who surrendered to God and continues to obey those in authority. After only six years as a Christian, he was ordained. We attended Bible college together and received theology degrees in 2004. The two of us have served in The Solid Rock Road ministry at Joy Christian Fellowship since 2002 and work with our pastors in leading the church.

We gave our lives to God and He has given our life back to us. I often think about how everything could have gone wrong if I didn't go with God or take a risk with my marriage to follow the path.

Today, nineteen of our children and grandchildren are with us at Joy, and one of our daughters is serving God at Jubilee Christian Fellowship in San Jose, California. We are an example of family salvation and restoration based on our commitment to staying on the path. ■

Justification by Faith
In Christian theology, "justification" is God's act of declaring or making a sinner righteous before God. Therefore, in the justification by faith process, God calls you righteous when you prove your faith.

Every test of faith counts on your journey towards sanctification. Along the way, God watches for three things: 1) how you react to the onset of a test; 2) how you act in the midst of the test; and 3) the outcome or the results of the test.

God pays attention when you resist a test and will put an alternative plan in place to give you another chance at being justified in your faith. When you're taking a detour, God will guide you back towards the path, but He won't force you back on it.

You may have to go through your cycle to get back on course—a huge waste of time and often a journey through hell. When the test is hard, God evaluates the level of trust you have in Him. If He sees you faltering, He often allows the heat to be turned up instead of rescuing you quickly and easing your pain.

> **You will be changed from the inside out, using God's strength to overcome your weaknesses and enacting His power to perform miracles.**

Of course, God's goal is for Christians to experience victory at the end of the test. When we stand on God's promise to move our mountains, and if we willingly suffer all the way to the cross with the right attitude, we will experience a faith-justifying victory.

James 1:2-4 shows us how we're to take tests: *"Consider it pure joy, my brothers, whenever you face trials of many kinds, because you know that the testing of your faith develops perseverance. Perseverance must finish its work so that you may be mature and complete, not lacking anything." (NIV)*

To enact faith, you must surrender to the will of God and have a real relationship with Him. In previous chapters, you learned the importance of Jesus being Lord, and how to pray and meditate on the Word of God. It's your responsibility to build yourself up spiritually. If you want a revelation from God to strengthen your faith, you must first be faithful.

Our faith grows as we see God in everything and practice His principles even when we don't know what the future holds.

True faith may begin small, but if you practice it, you will develop a permanent inner confidence in God that makes you sure of His existence and His love for you. You will be changed from the inside out, using God's strength to overcome your weaknesses and enacting His power to perform miracles.

Hebrews 11:1 says: *"Now faith is the substance of things hoped for, the evidence of things not seen...."* The question all Christians have to ask themselves is, "Can I believe something before I see it?" This doesn't come naturally because our experiences outside of God consistently prove that seeing is believing: whatever happens in the physical realm is the reality of the situation.

And yet, we can stand on Matthew 19:26: *"With men this is impossible, but with God all things are possible."* This scripture isn't a cliché. It's a Christian truth.

We can move the hand of God to enact His will. But here's the clincher. In Mark 9:23, Jesus says it this way: *"If you can believe, all things are possible to him who believes."* This adds the faith element.

Test of Sobriety

James 2:14-26 identifies two kinds of faith. One leads to godly works and one does not. The scriptures show that activated faith is true faith, while inactive, word-only faith is false. In other words, don't say you have faith when you don't plan on living as if what you say is your reality.

Here's your test. Can you tell the world that you'll never drink or do drugs again? If not, you have no faith in God's saving grace, His supernatural power, or His freeing work on the cross. If you don't believe you can have a lifetime of joyful sobriety, you won't have it.

On the other hand, if you're willing to tell everyone you know and anyone who will listen that you have quit using for the rest of your life, you are activating this reality. You're exhibiting true faith for never-ending sobriety. For this reason, we don't agree with a program that requires members to claim they are an alcoholic or drug addict every time they speak.

We do see the value in the one-day-at-time theology some people believe in. After all, Christianity is also mastered one day at time as described in Luke 9:23: *"'If anyone desires to come after Me, let him deny himself, and take up his cross daily, and follow Me."*

The difference is that Christians follow the model of Jesus who suffered all the way to the cross and finished the work.

Pope John Paul II said this about the cross: "When the cross is embraced it becomes a sign of love and of total self-giving. To carry it behind Christ means to be united with him in offering the greatest proof of love ... the choice is between a full life and an empty existence, between truth and falsehood."

God's blessings are not hit and miss. They're targeted to those who stay within the boundaries that the Bible describes in detail.

Sanctification

As Christians, we're supposed to enter the process of sanctification from the moment of salvation until the day of our physical death. In the literal sense, sanctification means to become useful to God.

This kind of news is not good for those who tend to be takers. One of the main reasons addicts stray from the path is they don't want to be used by God. Instead, they want to use God.

This is sad because it's true. We have watched so many people come and go because Christianity wasn't what they thought it should be, and God wasn't good enough to them. They asked for help, but expected God to do all the work, like a spiritual Santa Claus who drops off blessings on demand, whether someone is naughty or nice.

As your Father in heaven, God wants to bless you. But the ruler of the universe can't pour out His goodness on you if you're never within the blessing zone. God's blessings are not hit and miss. They're targeted to those who stay within the boundaries that the Bible describes in detail.

+ Marks the Spot

If you were on a treasure hunt, you would follow the exact path that leads to where + marks the spot. You'd be a fool to deviate from the directions that promise to take you right where you want to go. Why then do you deviate from God's path?

For God to use you, and in turn give you treasures from heaven, you must stay on the path and do what He says, to the letter. When you commit to that, you will go from having a saved-by-grace mentality to accepting the continual process of being justified by your faith that results in sanctification. Only then will you enter the blessing zone of God.

Right before Jesus was arrested, He prayed a beautiful prayer for His disciples. In John 17:15-17, the Son of God says to His Father, *"I do not pray that You should take them out of the world, but that You should keep them from the evil one. They are not of*

*the world, just as I am not of the world. Sanctify them
by Your truth. Your word is truth."*

Pay attention to this prayer because it shows where
+ marks the spot in terms of sanctification. It says we
will be sanctified when we know God's truth.
Therefore, we have to read the Bible to gain His
knowledge and receive revelation.

The Solid Rock Road is one of many sanctification
processes. If you follow the path, you'll experience
radical transformation and discover treasures beyond
your wildest dreams. But your walk with God
continues well after you've read this book, so get ready
for your next sanctification challenge.

Perfection

Mankind is imperfect, but God set the standard of
Christianity as perfection using Himself and Jesus as
models. In Matthew 5:48, Jesus says, *"Therefore you
shall be perfect, just as your Father in heaven is
perfect."* In this scripture, Jesus is referring to our
capacity for love. He tells us that the more we love, the
more perfect we are in God's eyes.

As you strive for perfection in the area of love, you
can also consider the value in having a perfect heart
towards God. Since the heart has a tendency to be
wicked and deceitful according to scripture, the
condition of your heart is a serious matter. Read
Psalms and you'll understand what it means to have a
heart connection with God.

A Single Path

There is only one path ordained by God. He didn't set
up alternative courses to choose from. This is contrary
to our natural mind and goes against New Age
thinking, which claims that all roads lead to God. And,
it surely doesn't jive with our fears or free-thinking
self-will that is determined on doing our own thing.

If you're a new Christian or it has taken you a long time to find the right path, then God is not going to ask something of you that you can't do. Yet, He is famous for asking more of us than we're already giving, and for asking us to move forward on the path even when we're comfortable right where we are.

A Note on the Biblical Use of Alcohol

It's not a sin to enjoy a glass of wine or a beer, but scripture after scripture warns us about the dangers of too much alcohol. Many Biblical stories describe the costly mistakes of drunkenness.

For example, when Noah drank too much wine from his vineyard, he passed out and got naked in front of his sons. Lot got so drunk at night that he blacked out while his two daughters had sex with him on consecutive evenings.

When you drink, you lose your resolve, you act recklessly, and more often than not, you drink more than you intended. It only takes a few too many to say things you don't mean, have sex when you vow not to, or spend money you don't have. You might drive a vehicle and end up with a DUII, have an accident, or run over and kill a pedestrian.

With any level of intoxication, you can change your life forever – and for the worse.

Through personal experience, and having heard just about everything there is to hear as counselors, we feel secure in saying, it is best not to drink alcohol in any form, ever.

We use Proverbs 23:29-35 as a scripture reference when explaining the seduction, the misery and the consequences of alcohol abuse. You can also translate this into drug abuse. When you read this, you will understand the position God takes on drunkenness and you won't have any doubt that he realizes the depth of the temptation.

"Who has Woe?
Who has sorrow?
Who has contentions?
Who has complaints?
Who has redness of eyes?
Those who linger long at the wine,
Those who go in search of mixed wine.
Do not look on the wine when it is red,
When it sparkles in the cup,
When it swirls around smoothly;
At the last it bites like a serpent,
And stings like a viper.
Your eyes will see strange things,
And your heart will utter perverse things.
Yes, you will be like one who lies down
in the midst of the sea,
Or like one who lies at the top of the mast, saying
"They have struck me, but I was not hurt;
They have beaten me, but I did not feel it.
When shall I awake, that I may seek another
drink?"

Accept Challenges

As this chapter closes, we ask you to accept the challenges God places in your path, and to overcome the obstacles Satan puts in your way. If you stay on course, you'll remain within God's blessing zone and end up where + marks the spot. You'll discover your destiny.

By the way, Christianity is not all work. There is a lot of fun and plenty of surprises along The Solid Rock Road. We have a blast being sober. The best part is that we get to remember everything we said and did!

Principle 9: Be Ready for Battle— Put on the Full Armor of God

"Finally, my brethren, be strong in the Lord and in the power of His might. Put on the whole armor of God, that you may be able to stand against the wiles of the devil. For we do not wrestle against flesh and blood, but against principalities, against powers, against the rulers of the darkness of this age, against spiritual hosts of wickedness in the heavenly places. Therefore take up the whole armor of God, that you may be able to withstand in the evil day, and having done all, to stand."
— Ephesians 6:10-13

In the early days of our Christianity, our pastor and leaders kept telling us to fight the battle when all we really wanted to do was rest. We had been exhausted from living our sinful lives. As you well know, it's a lot of work managing things in the midst of your addiction.

The constant battle to survive took all our energy in those days. We had to feed our children and keep a roof over their heads. When there was a relationship going on, we were either fighting unworthy battles to keep our men from leaving, or trying to create a sense of harmony when there wasn't a hint of it. We also had to stay high, which isn't easy when you're nearly broke.

For many years, we had to fight just to wake up and face our day. Without a good plan, we inched forward and made life happen by the skin of our teeth.

Anyone who has fought these kinds of battles on a daily basis knows how hard it is to keep building a life from nothing. It's exhausting to keep things together as sin and addiction tear them apart.

There were times when the two of us barely had enough money to make ends meet, but bought weed instead of paying some already late bills or rent. We figured the drug was essential for reducing money-related stress.

While this strategy worked and the marijuana served its intended purposes, an eighth of an ounce would quickly run dry and with it, all hope of being content and calm. Depression then became an unbearable weight and all we could think to do was buy more pot and drink more alcohol, and put another bill or two aside for payment at a later date.

In between the pot and alcohol, we treated ourselves to harder drugs, depending on availability and our moods. Neither of us knows how we escaped being completely strung out on speed, but we can assure you, it had nothing to do with our being smarter or more strategic than anyone else.

Christian Soldiers

Every human has to fight battles. The question is, which battle is worth your energy? Will you fight as a soldier in the Army of God where you're equipped and supported, and where the umbrella of protection remains open? Or will you insist on being a lone

Christian who stands defenseless against the barrage of life?

If you were a soldier in the United States Army, you would be considered a fool if you went into the battlefield alone and unarmed. You would either be killed, taken prisoner, or face serious reprimand by your commanding officer. But if you refused to fight altogether and went AWOL, you would be a deserter and found guilty of treason.

Treason is a crime in which a person betrays an oath of loyalty and in some way willfully cooperates with an enemy. Anyone guilty of treason is called a traitor, which is defined on Dictionary.com as "someone who says one thing and does another."

When you call yourself a Christian but act like a drunken, drugged-out heathen, you're treasonous.

Standing

We are astounded at the number of recovering addicts who tell us they relapsed because the lifestyle of an addict is easier than a Christian. Truthfully, when we hear this, our initial responses are not very Christian-like or counselor-like. We have to hold ourselves back from screaming out, "Have you lost your mind?"

We have to activate the Spirit of God within us so we can think and act from a spiritual perspective.

After one episode in which a relapsed Christian whined about Christianity being too hard, we realized that he hadn't lost his mind, but had instead lost the mind of Christ. He forgot that the battles fought in the Spirit didn't have to be won in his own strength. Satan lied to him and he believed it.

Ephesians 6:10-18 starts with: *"...be strong in the Lord and the power of His might."* It ends with, *"...and having done all, to stand."*

We can only stand in the midst of a battle if we have God's strength, power, and protection. We are only protected and powerful if we put on the Armor of God. We can only put on the armor if we set our mind to such a mission. For that, we need the mind of Christ, which is found in the Bible, through prayer, and by enacting the work of the Holy Spirit.

Simply put, we have to activate the Spirit of God within us so we can think and act from a spiritual perspective. When we have the mind of Christ, we are able to use God's intelligence and His supernatural muscles to win every round in the boxing match of life. We can stand and face the enemy!

Going AWOL

A lot of people don't want to be in a war. They seek peace, but choose to sit out the spiritual fight. Instead of standing, they waver and often fall.

On the other hand, these same people will fight like trained pit bulls for their earthly rights to self-rule, and to get high. They are ruthless when it comes to getting a fix.

People who turn away from God and give up the fight become AWOL in God's army. In doing so, they often find ways to justify themselves and come against the Word of God. Most of the time, they get offended by those in authority over them. Their actions and their words convict them of treason, yet they continue claiming their Christianity under the umbrella of grace.

When AWOL, you're no longer accessing the mind of Christ but are operating with your human mind and in your flesh. This is not a good place to be.

Romans 8:6-8 says this: *"For to be carnally minded is death, but to be spiritually minded is life and peace.*

Because the carnal mind is enmity against God; for it is not subject to the law of God, nor indeed can be. So then, those who are in the flesh cannot please God."

The above scripture comes from the Apostle Paul who clearly states that your natural mind opposes, or even hates, God. He takes it a few steps further by saying you are an outlaw when you aren't in the Spirit, and offensive to God.

It's less of an insult to God if you admit you're AWOL, rather than deny it and try to convince yourself and others you're still on spiritual duty. It's better to acknowledge you have taken off your armor, laid down your weapons, and are hunkering down in a bunker. Don't pretend you're standing firm and ready for spiritual battle when you aren't.

Whether you come clean or not, the fact remains that without God's protection, you can't stand against the "wiles of the devil." When you fake it, the devil gets the upper hand and proves you can't do it.

Many people think the devil is simply the manifestation of evil, but he is as crafty as he is wicked. That's why he's able to consistently make a mockery of your life. I'm sure you don't question that the devil tempts you to use drugs and alcohol and that once you consume them, evil abounds.

But in 2 Corinthians 11:14, the Apostle Paul says that the devil has many faces, including the persona of an angel of light. In Revelation, he is called a deceiver and an accuser. In the Gospel of John, Jesus refers to the devil as the father of lies, and in Genesis, the serpent is described as subtle.

We have to watch out for the devil's quiet, clever tactics. If he gains a single foothold over you, he is well on his way to gaining a stronghold. He'll start with having you question the Word of God, then fill you with lies to replace the truth. In your confusion and compromise, he'll bring deception that gets a hold of you and won't let go until there's a moment of clarity and the truth is revealed once again.

It's no wonder so many Christians are two-faced where God is concerned. One day we think He's amazing, and the next we're asking ourselves if heaven exists. Have you ever floated in the Spirit, then been so deep in darkness that you deny the Spirit altogether?

> **The only cure for schizophrenic Christianity is to trade it for the single-mindedness of the Spirit.**

In relapse mode, nothing is really right, but wrong things can seem appropriate. And those who have succumbed to addictions after failing to remain in the truth either call out to God for help in desperation or curse Him because He did not come to the rescue on their terms.

Satan loves the misery of people on the verge of relapse, or in the midst of it. There is so much torment for half-hearted Christians who straddle the fence, swaying between guilt and forgiveness, condemnation and conviction, grace and judgment, peace and chaos, self-hate and self-love, and every other Christian yin and yang.

The only cure for schizophrenic Christianity is to trade it for the single-mindedness of the Spirit. When you access the mind of Christ, you know the truth and it sets you free. But when you refuse to become a soldier in God's army, you go AWOL and become a traitor. You say one thing but do another. You play both sides of the street and thereby deceive yourselves and others. You are a help to no one, except the enemy.

True soldiers of God stand firm and protect the home front. Deserters flee, leaving themselves and their loved ones open to the harsh elements of the world.

 Galatians 5:24 says that if we're in Christ, we have crucified the flesh with its passions and desires. The result is that we are free and happy.

You may experience snippets of happiness when you're high, but they're fleeting. We recall having a great time at parties, only to go to bed feeling bad and waking up feeling worse.

Galatians 5:19-21 provides a list of 17 emotions and actions that are evidence of our sin nature at work. Drunkenness, contentions, dissensions, outbursts of wrath, and revelries are among this list.

Verse 21 says that those who practice one or more items from the bad fruit list will not inherit the kingdom of God. We suggest you read all of Galatians 5 and ask yourself which kind of fruit you're growing in your spiritual greenhouse.

Also, write down the answers to the questions below. Dig deep so God can reveal any issues you have in relation to this Principle.

- In what ways am I a soldier or a deserter?
- What steps do I need to take that will help me to enter and stand in the battle?
- Am I using the mind of Christ and seeing life from a spiritual perspective or am I using my own mind?
- How is my prayer life? Am I praying *to* God or am I interacting *with* God?
- Has my church attendance been regular, or have I found excuses to miss services here and there?
- Am I currently active in open sin, or is there hidden sin I need to be aware of? Am I willing to repent?
- Do I experience torment as a Christian? If so, why am I not at peace?

What is the Battle?

In this chapter, we refer to the battle, not the war. This is purposeful because the war was won when the Son of God suffered to the cross and died on it. The words "It is finished," were Jesus' last words and a victory statement for Christians.

Now you may ask, "If the war has already been won, why is it necessary to be ready for battle, and why battle at all?" The answer is that battles are often fought for the sake of continued peace. The United States military doesn't take a breather or dissolve itself in times of peace; it actually builds itself up and uses peace time to get stronger and smarter.

If you seek peace, you have to become a spiritual warrior. When you do, you will learn godly methods for controlling your mind and actions. You will also learn how to defend yourself against the devil's vicious attacks, and his sneaky little intrusions into your life.

Fighting is not always pleasant, but if you don't fight to stay in the light now, you'll have to fight your way out of the dark later.

Don't worry that the battle is too hard or fear that you'll tire out in the middle of it. When you use the strength of God and the mind of Christ, you can go the distance while experiencing peace in the battle. Along the way, you get comfort and counsel from the Holy Spirit, as well as support from fellow soldiers in the Army of God.

The Training

New recruits in the United States Army are expected to quickly attach to the organization's written vision, which is "Relevant and Ready Landpower in Service to the Nation." They then embark on a nine-week journey that transforms them from a civilian to a full-fledged soldier.

Along the way, soldiers learn rules and regulations. They undergo tests of physical and mental endurance.

They accept challenges to accomplish what they don't believe they can, employing a mind-over-matter mentality. And they are taught to use weapons, with the goal of achieving Marksman status.

Soldiers in boot camp bond with fellow recruits and learn the art of teamwork. They march together and go the distance. Trainers take their men into the field, where they practice newly learned combat skills. Finally, each soldier discovers their strengths and consistently increases their proficiency.

The Army of God is much the same. When you join, you will embark on a lifelong journey that transforms you from an unsaved sinner to a full-fledged Christian soldier. When you sober up and stay straight, you have passed the first test of physical and mental endurance. However, your stamina will be re-tested over and over again.

As a combat-ready Christian, you can protect yourself against your enemy, and you will be taking your skills to the street.

If you don't go AWOL, you'll embrace the laws of God and become attached to God's vision for your clean and sober life. *"Therefore, if anyone is in Christ, he is a new creation; old things have passed away; behold all things have become new."* (2 Corinthians 5:17).

With this mandate, you can incorporate the Army's mind-over-matter mentality to achieve the impossible and manifest the miraculous.

While in training, you learn to use spiritual weapons of warfare. You'll become an expert at wielding the sword of the Spirit and guarding yourself with the shield of Faith. As a combat-ready Christian, you can protect yourself against your enemy, and you will be taking your skills to the street, helping to rescue the unsaved and the backslidden.

Meanwhile, you're allowing God to reveal your spiritual strengths. Remember, you don't determine your gifts, you discover them as you seek the will of God, as described in Principle 7. This process happens as you get ready for battle and continue your training.

The true secret to success in God's Army is constant surrender and submission to God's vision. Everything begins and ends with these two acts. If you aren't surrendered and submitted, you will engage in the wrong battle.

As Ephesians 6:12 states, we're not battling against flesh and blood, rather Satan and his evil spirits. The trick Satan plays is to create conflict with people in your life, whether it's your family, friends, spiritual leaders, or members of your church.

If the devil succeeds in creating conflict and offenses, your rebellion kicks in. Rebellion is simply self-will, which usually results in your relapse.

Prisoners of War

You can become the devil's prisoner of war when you go AWOL in the Army of God. You often premeditate your surrender to the devil. But once behind evil bars, you're at Satan's mercy, although mercy is not in him. Ultimately, you are denied even the basics of survival.

In the natural world, rules govern the treatment of POWs, but the devil doesn't care about your humanity. He will torture you, force you into hard labor, deliberately starve you, beat you down, withhold relationships, interrogate you, lie to you, and manipulate your circumstances. As a spiritual POW, you are so weakened that you can't think clearly and the devil's lies become your truth.

You must hate being a captive more than you love self-will. You have every key you need to open the doors to your personal prison and get out for good. Will you use them and be free once and for all?"

If you hate being captive more than you love it, you'll use any means possible to escape.

We can hear you saying, "It's not that simple." But we never said it was. If you hate being captive more than you love it, you'll use any means possible to escape. If you love it more than you hate it, you'll find a million excuses to remain the devil's hostage.

There is no shortage of excuses when it comes to addiction. However, Ephesians 6:14-17 provides a battle plan that ensures your ability to escape from captivity and offers continued freedom through truth, righteousness, preparation, faith, a renewed mind, and the knowledge of God.

"Stand therefore, having girded your waist with truth, having put on the breastplate of righteousness, and having shod your feet with the preparation of the gospel of peace; above all, taking the shield of faith with which you will be able to quench all the fiery darts of the wicked one. And take the helmet of salvation, and the sword of the Spirit, which is the word of God."

Below are brief explanations relating to the Armor of God. We're keeping it simple on purpose because our main goal is to help you understand the importance of putting on each piece of armor. It's your responsibility to discover the details in the armor.

Put on the Belt of Truth

You should be seeking to know the truth your entire Christian walk. If you have trouble separating truth from lies, you fall into deception and trade the truth for a lie. Things can go downhill rather quickly when that happens. For you, deception can be deadly.

In 2 Timothy 2:25-26, the Apostle Paul says we are to correct those who are in opposition to the truth and pray that God will grant them repentance so they will *"escape the snare of the devil, having been taken captive by him to do his will."*

The only way to escape the snare is to know the truth by reading the Bible and accessing the mind of Christ. When all is said and done, being skilled in the Word is what will keep you in the truth, help you stay on God's path, and transform you into a combat-ready soldier in the Army of God.

To know the truth is good, but you must come to love and crave it, the same way you have been obsessed by your drug of choice. If you make this switch in your mind, your body will follow.

Some people experience love at first sight with truth, while others grow to love it. If you have an instant connection with truth, this does not save you from deception later down the road. You have to nurture your relationship with the knowledge of God.

If you're not automatically captivated by truth, don't despair. If you keep searching for God's truth, you'll find it!

No matter how you come to love the truth, it will become part of you. When you operate in truth, you have better insight into the spiritual battle facing you. When you're in deception, you can't see your invisible enemy. That's why the devil tries to prevent you from knowing the truth, often steals your truth, and covers it up. If you're blind to the wiles of the devil, he can get away with his schemes more often than not.

It bears repeating that the truth will set you free. This truth comes in two forms: First you must be truthful about your addictions, your cycles, your thoughts, and your feelings or you will continue drinking and doing drugs. Secondly, you must know God's truth, which gives an internal peace and guides you along The Solid Rock Road.

Also, Matthew 7:24-25 says that the truth will bring stability to those who hear and obey it. According to the Gospel of John, truth gives life and it sanctifies and purifies. The Psalms have much to say on the subject of truth. For example, David writes in Psalm 119:105 that truth endures, it gives us hope, makes the simple wise and it is *"a lamp unto our feet and a light unto our path."*

Wear the Breastplate of Righteousness
In the old days, the breastplate was another word for neck-to-thigh body armor which provided Roman soldiers protection for major vital organs, including the heart. Since we know that by nature, *"the heart is deceitful above all things, and desperately wicked."* (Jeremiah 17:9), the breastplate of righteousness must be worn at all times or your softened heart will harden.

The breastplate is Christ's righteousness. It allows Christians the ability to become right before God.

The breastplate of righteousness also protects your heart against emotional pain. The devil always tries to re-open scars of your past and create new hurts so you can remain a victim of wrongdoing. He wants you to forget that Jesus died so you can be completely healed and live in victory.

Shod Your Feet
Roman foot soldiers took off their armor to rest between battles, but they left their shoes on. And they wore well-made shoes with a lot of support and traction so they could stand longer, march further, and remain on their feet while performing hand-to-hand combat.

When you shod your feet with the preparation of the Gospel of peace, you quickly respond to an attack from the enemy, and you walk boldly in the ways of God. As you walk with confidence, you're ready to share the Good News and teach people how the finished work at the cross is a benefit. This requires you to read the Bible, meditate on the Word, and pray for understanding as you learned in earlier Principles.

> ▶ You can't talk confidently about the good things of God if you haven't overcome your addictions, or at least accepted the challenge to do so.

Romans 10:15 says, *"How beautiful are the feet of those who preach the gospel of peace, who bring glad tidings of good things."*

You can't talk confidently about the good things of God if you haven't overcome your addictions, or at least accepted the challenge to do so. The goal is for you to have a walking testimony of standing firm in your convictions and declaring yourself free.

The Shield of Faith

Faith acts like a shield to deflect fear and doubt. We know it's a valuable spiritual weapon because the word 'faith' appears 245 times in the New Testament. Combined, these scriptures help us understand what faith is, and how to attain and activate it.

Generally, faith is having confidence that God is who He says He is. By its very nature, faith requires Christians to believe something that is not yet fact. When fully developed, faith results in our needs being met and our dreams unfolding – all for God's glory.

When it comes to faith, God doesn't want you to speak empty words or Christian clichés. Instead, He wants to see true demonstrations of your complete trust in Him. Hebrews 11:1 says, *"Now faith is being sure of what we hope for and certain of what we do not see." (NIV)*

 Demonstration of Faith

A great example of faith occurred in 2005 when my husband Jerry got word from God that he was to go on a mission trip to Vera Cruz, Mexico. Since Jerry had never felt called to missions, this was a surprise and he initially resisted.

Later that year, our pastor announced there was a mission trip scheduled for Vera Cruz the following January. This was confirmation that Jerry should go, but he got even more proof when a missions calling was spoken over him during his ordination ceremony. Right then, Jerry set his Vera Cruz traveling plans in stone.

The morning the missions group was to depart, Jerry ended up in the hospital. He was bleeding internally from an eroded esophagus and the doctor's report was, "He's a very sick man, He'll be with us for a while."

I adamantly told the nurse and doctor that Jerry was leaving for a mission trip that day. They told me he wasn't. I told them that God had confirmed his Mexico appointment. They responded with medical terminology and began the process of admittance.

When they wheeled Jerry upstairs and into a hospital room, I felt a seed of doubt begin to sprout. I prayed and asked, "God, you don't change your mind, so what am I to think about all this?" The Holy Spirit answered, saying, "Jerry is to be a sign and a wonder in this place."

Faith restored, I affirmed to the nurse that Jerry was going on a mission to Vera Cruz. The nurse remained polite, but quickly changed the subject. Soon, Jerry was in with the surgeon who was using a medical process to identify where the bleeding was coming from, and to make plans for surgery.

My friend, Jan, showed up at the hospital as I waited for the doctor's latest report. We prayed for God's will to be done. When the doctor emerged, he said, "The bleeding has stopped."

"So what does that mean? What happens from here?" I asked the doctor.

"There's nothing to do surgically, but he'll have to take Prilosec every day for the rest of his life, and we'll need to watch him for a while."

Jan called our pastor who was on his way to the Portland Airport with the rest of the mission group.

"What do we do now?" she asked.

"Jerry will know what to do," the pastor assured her.

Back in his room, Jerry was completely coherent when we walked in. "What's the story?" he asked.

"The bleeding stopped. You need to take Prilosec..."

"That's it?" Jerry interrupted, as he turned toward the nurse. "You need to get these tubes out of me now because I'm going to Vera Cruz."

At that, Jan got on the phone and made reservations for an eight o'clock flight out of Medford, which would have him arrive in Portland before the midnight flight to Vera Cruz. But by seven that night, the fog rolled into Medford and fifteen minutes before the plane was to take off, the flight got cancelled.

But that didn't stop Jerry. The next morning, he boarded the first plane out of Medford, and eventually met up with the mission group in Vera Cruz. Having just held up the Shield of Faith, Jerry had the opportunity to lay hands on many poor families he met during the outreach portion of the mission.

Faith overcomes fear and eliminates doubt. Whenever God gives you a word or scripture, you have to believe God over Satan who wants to void the truth and power of it.

A month or so after this incident, I got a call from the finance department of the hospital who wanted to find out about our insurance. He said, "I heard about your husband going to Mexico. That's quite a remarkable story. People are talking about it around here." This confirmed that Jerry was truly a sign and a wonder that day.

Sometimes we have more faith in the devil than we do in God. We're sure Satan exists and is able to mess up our life and talk us into doing things we don't want to do.

Learn to stand on your faith. You may not see God in the midst of your trouble, but He really is present, working your life out according to His divine plan. ∎

Helmet of Salvation

The Helmet of Salvation protects your mind from worldly thoughts and reminds you that you have been saved by the blood of Jesus. Like a child who rides a bike, the helmet protects from impact and trauma to the brain.

The Helmet of Salvation keeps you in your right mind. When you wear it, the devil's lies will have no impact and whatever he throws your way can't penetrate and cause injury. The helmet is your spiritual thinking cap, ensuring you retain the mind of Christ.

The Helmet of Salvation helps you win the battle of your mind. It keeps you settled and peaceful, and ensures you stay spiritually balanced and focused. Without it, your mind runs amuck and sucks up the images and reasoning of the world.

The Sword of the Spirit

The sword is the major offensive weapon of God's warfare. In Principle 3, you learned how important it is to pray and meditate on the Word of God daily. Since the Sword of the Spirit is the Word of God, everything written in the Bible can be used as a weapon to overcome the devil.

Since the devil doesn't have the Spirit of God in him, he is defenseless against the Word. Hebrews 4:12 says, *"For the word of God is living and powerful, and sharper than any two-edged sword..."*

When you wield the sword appropriately, you cut the devil in a million pieces. You have to picture yourself cutting away at his lies, accusations, and temptations by quoting scripture. That's what Jesus did while He was in the desert for forty days. Read up on this section of the Bible.

 Since the Word of God is your best offensive weapon, you must use it if you want victory.

In Matthew 4:4,7 and 10, Jesus' response to the devil's temptations started with *"It is written."* This should be your response when tempted to use drugs or alcohol. If you gather several scriptures listed in Principle 3 and wield the Sword of the Spirit, you'll be amazed at how quickly you win the battle.

Since the Word of God is your best offensive weapon, you must use it if you want victory. Otherwise you're in a constant defensive state, which gets you nowhere and keeps you feeling like a victim who is barely able to ward off your attacker.

Remember, the sword was designed for hand-to-hand combat. So take it and use it. The more you pick it up and the more you use this powerful weapon, the more dangerous to the devil you become.

The Daily Armor Prayer

We put on the Armor of God every morning. Many Solid Rock Road graduates learn how to discern when they are armed and dangerous against the enemy and when they are weak and vulnerable.

Your goal is to get your armor on before your day starts. If you don't get it on early, you may not get it on at all.

Get in the habit of putting on the Armor of God before you get out of bed. When we access God's DNA and get our selfish, self-centered sin nature out of the way, good things happen.

During one of our Solid Rock Road groups, a young woman named Beth told a story about how her parents taught the family to say an Armor of God prayer. Beth isn't an addict but chose to go through the program to overcome fears and move to the next level of her Christian walk. For our benefit, Beth typed up her family's prayer. Ever since, we have handed it out to participants in our Solid Rock Road groups.

With Beth's permission, and with love to those who are reading this book, we present this awesome prayer to you. Feel free to memorize or copy it, then read it aloud every morning. When you do, you're preparing for daily battle. You are also accessing the mind of Christ, God's DNA, and the power of the Holy Spirit. You can never go wrong with that combination.

Stand Therefore, having girded your waist with the truth

Thank you Lord for your truth. You are truth and You alone set me free from sin and lies. Today, I choose to believe and put on the truth about who You are and who I am as Your child. Holy Spirit, lead and guide my thoughts in Your path of truth. Help me to make wise decisions today based on Your word. Help me to speak the truth in love to myself and others. And give me discernment so I know when people are speaking truth and when Satan is using lies to get me off the path.

Having put on the breastplate of righteousness

Thank You, God, for Your breastplate of righteousness. I put it on and it covers me today. In the name of Jesus, I take off any robes of self-righteousness or works of the law that would glorify me and distract me from the finished work of Jesus at the cross. I ask you, Lord, to help me maintain my heart with diligence, for out of it flow the issues of life.

And having shod your feet with the preparation of the gospel of peace
Thank You, Father, for Your good news of peace to me. I put on Your gospel of peace. May my steps be secure and protected today. Prepare me to speak to others about Your love and the good things You've done in my life. Help me to live in peace and walk as a peacemaker.

Above all, taking the shield of faith with which you will be able to quench all the fiery darts of the wicked one
Father, You are a shield about me and the glory and the lifter of my head. I want to please you, Lord, with my faith in You. You're my Savior, though I don't always see what You are doing, or plan to do. My trust in You puts You between my enemy and me. I am forever secure in You and inaccessible to Satan.

And take the helmet of salvation
Father, thank You for saving me from sin and death. I receive Your gift of salvation, deliverance, and healing. I have the mind of Christ and I can do all things through Christ who strengthens me. Help me to think pure thoughts and praise You. Thank You for making me a new creation. Make my mind new, and help me not to be ignorant of Satan's plans.

And the sword of the Spirit, which is the word of God
Father, thank You for the weapon of Your Word and Your Spirit. When the enemy comes to steal, kill, or destroy me, quicken scripture to me so I can stand. May my sword (God's Word) be exercised to defeat the enemy today. In the name of Jesus, Amen.

In Summary
In the final Solid Rock Road group, we offer victory statements to participants following the 'Be Ready for

Battle' session. We ask that they find and use a scripture as a foundation for their freedom from addictions. We're always amazed at how encouraging and empowering these scriptures can be.

While you know that you're supposed to have the victory, we believe it's time you really did.

Below are scriptures with victory statements. Choose one that suits you best, then write it or type it out and put the scripture on your refrigerator as a reminder that you've won!

- Romans 8:37-39
- I Corinthians 15:57
- Proverbs 2:6-8
- Psalms 118:13-15
- Psalms 60:12
- Psalms 44:4-7
- Psalms 18:32-35
- 2 Corinthians 10:4,5
- 2 Timothy 4:18
- 2 Corinthians 12:9
- Isaiah 41:13
- 1 John 4:4

Isn't it great to be on the winning team?

Principle 10: Serve God and Others

"For you, brethren, have been called to liberty; only
do not use liberty as an opportunity for the flesh,
but through love serve one another."
— Galatians 5:13

Sometimes we daydream that we're living on an island and lying around in hammocks under the shade of palm trees. With the snap of a finger, a tray of fresh fruit and colorful drinks with umbrellas arrive at our side. With a soft wind blowing by and no cares in the world, we savor sweet melon and sip on alcohol-free Piña Coladas.

But we don't live on an island. We live in Medford, Oregon, where palm trees don't grow naturally. Neither of us owns a hammock and the only colorful drink we've had this week is pre-sweetened Cherry Cool-Aid made for the grandkids.

Don't get us wrong. We believe in taking vacations, especially ocean cruises with never-ending access to fresh fruit from a buffet and where room service happily delivers a feast with refreshments. But our team is on a mission to deliver a message of freedom, and it requires that we get active.

In our neighborhood, we see hurt and dying generations of people held hostage by their foolish choices in the darkened hallways of drug addiction and alcoholism. Everywhere we look and everywhere we go, our hearts break and our resolve grows.

Together and separately, The Solid Rock Road team grabs people out of the fire, out of their fear, and out of self-made prisons. We celebrate freedom, but only long enough to identify new captives and help unlock another prison door.

For many years, we have waged war on the enemy of man's soul. And though the focus is on deliverance from drugs and alcohol, we have accepted the assignment to teach, rebuke, inspire, educate, and guide the unsaved and those active in sin of any kind.

A Radical Message

Some people call this message of freedom we preach 'radical.' But drastic measures of truth are absolutely necessary with the world in its present condition and people blindly walking along the Yellow Brick Road where danger, disappointment, and hell await.

We've made it clear throughout this book that the teachings in The Solid Rock Road are based solely on scripture. We refuse to water down God's Word, or to add to it. Unfortunately, this seems radical to most people, including many Christians.

Yet every hero in the Bible stepped out of mediocrity and became an extremist to free themselves and others from slavery, idolatry, immorality, and a long list of ungodly behaviors and circumstances.

We could provide many examples of godly exploits described in the Bible. Noah built an Ark and saved himself, seven family members, the entire animal kingdom and the human race from total distinction. His neighbors thought he was insane as he built the massive boat, but Noah knew he had heard the voice of God and so he did as he was told.

Moses led his people out of Egyptian captivity, believing God could save them, but not necessarily knowing how. Moses didn't realize God planned to part the Red Sea or that God would present the Ten Commandments, but Moses did as he was instructed and miracles happened.

The Apostle Paul suffered imprisonment for his straightforward style of preaching. He didn't care how he sent the Gospel message around the then-known world. Paul only knew he must.

The service and actions of each of these heroes could help define the word 'radical,' but Jesus is the prime example of a Biblical extremist. Because Jesus loved mankind, He went straight for the root of sin. Some who encountered the Messiah were cut to the heart and repented, while others further hardened their hearts toward God.

Either way, Jesus dealt with their responses by moving forward in His ministry. He didn't beg people to believe or to obey. He simply provided the straight truth, then moved on and continued serving.

Jesus advocated and practiced self-denial, which is the true essence of love.

In Mark 10:45, the real purpose of Jesus' ministry is revealed: *"For even the Son of Man did not come to be served, but to serve, and to give His life as a ransom for many."* As God's Son, Jesus could have reveled in His title, or sent His disciples where He didn't want to go. Jesus could have built the world's largest congregation in one of His favorite cities. But instead, He humbly served His Father in heaven. And, He exhibited radical love through radical acts of service.

Jesus advocated and practiced self-denial, which is the true essence of love. In the midst of rejection and persecution, Jesus served, proving that love prevails in any circumstance.

How often do you deny your personal needs for the sake of others? How much of yourself do you willingly give to those who don't necessarily like you? It's easy to care for and serve people who admire you, but God's kind of love gives without expecting anything in return.

Luke 6:32-33 makes this point: *"But if you love those who love you, what credit is that to you? ... And if you do good to those who do good to you, what credit is that to you? For even sinners do the same..."*

As a Christian, you're called to a standard that extends beyond human nature. Ultimately, your love and service to others mirrors the condition of your heart. The goal as you walk along The Solid Rock Road is to soften your heart according to the Word, and in so doing, soften your heart toward the lost and toward Christians in need of your help.

A hard heart cannot model Christ, nor can it serve without selfish intent.

Read the Gospels

If you have never studied the life of Jesus (Mathew, Mark, Luke, and John), do so immediately, starting with the book of John.

If you're learning the 'how-to' of recovery but your heart isn't changing, then you're missing the mark by a long shot. In Luke 12:34, Jesus says: *"For where your treasure is, there your heart will be also."*

If you love attention and require it be given to you, then you will look for it wherever you go. You are self-absorbed and your heart is set on self-satisfaction. Your happiness is determined by how many people are listening to your woes, paying attention to your needs, and offering help and handouts.

Christianity Defined

To fully understand the ministry and character of Jesus, you must study what is written about His life. If you have no interest in reading the Bible or enacting the truth it presents, then you may have to quit referring to yourself as a Christian.

Wikipedia defines the word 'Christian' as "a follower of Jesus of Nazareth, referred to as Christ." The first known usage of this term is found in Acts 11:26: *"The disciples were first called Christians at Antioch."* *(NIV)*

If disciples are Christians, who are the rest of the people sitting in church? Since all scripture is given by inspiration of God, then He is very precise and limited in His definition of the word 'Christian.' And if you go by the verse in Acts, you can't claim the term if you're not a disciple.

Disciples follow the teachings of Christ. They live and look differently from the rest of the world. They reflect the character of Christ and through godly compassion, reach out into the world. Their actions, also known as their works, become a snapshot of their heart.

Observe the mannerisms, actions, and life of a Christian who serves God and others. You'll see a smile on their face and contentment in their speech. These servants don't complain when they go through hard times. In times of trouble, they're looking forward to understanding the lessons they will learn through the experience.

Servants of God don't stop serving because they're having problems. They keep doing the will of God no matter what. Some make it look easy, but what true servants know is that the end is always better than the beginning and that God always shows up and turns our tests into our testimonies.

From a Raging Fire to Ashes

We have seen a lot of people get saved and go after God with gusto. Christians call this 'being on fire.' These newborns can't stop talking about God, and their contagious enthusiasm draws friends and family to church, resulting in many additional salvations and new fires.

We get upset when we see the fire reduced to a small flame, then to a tiny flicker of light. Even still, we have hope because the flicker can ignite once again, and it often does!

But when we watch the raging fire die until all that's left are ashes, we get mad because we know Satan had a hand in it. He starts by watering down the Word, and continues by smothering the fire with lies, offenses, and euphoric recall in regard to drugs and alcohol.

Satan's hope is that your passion for God turns into a thirst for evil. And he often gets his way with you. But don't you dare blame it all on the devil! In order for you to relapse, you have to be in cahoots with him.

If all you see are dark remnants of your life, your ashes can provide the way for new spiritual growth – the same as in a burnt-out forest.

Up to now, you may have been ignorant or misinformed regarding the battle. But in previous chapters, you learned that there are three forces at work in your Christian life: God, the devil, and you. We know what God wants, we know what the devil wants, the question is, what do you want?

Check your flame. Is it still flickering? If so, then allow your passion to re-ignite through acts of godly compassion and service. If all you see are dark remnants of your life, your ashes can provide the way for new spiritual growth—the same way as in a burned-out forest. Thankfully, new growth will emerge the minute you repent and get back on the path to continue your journey of hope.

The Race

Marathon runners know it's never how they start the race, it's how they finish that counts. When we were in our twenties, we would sometimes go to the horse races with our parents. We considered this a unique and fun family outing. It cost $2 to bet on a horse, so we took $20 each and packed a lunch for a full day of action. (For the record, we don't believe in gambling and don't promote horse racing as an activity for Christians.)

Before each race, we decided which horse we thought would win the race. My mother, father, and brother studied the racing forms long and hard before choosing the horse they favored. But we would place bets according to our intuition. We cared most about the name of the horse and we had a thing for the least likely to succeed. We liked the idea of winning big with our small $2 investment.

A few seconds before each race, our family would stand in anticipation. As the gates opened and the announcer proclaimed, "And they're off," each of us zeroed in on the horse we chose to win.

Sometimes our horse would jump out of the gate and lead the way for quite a while. As we rooted that rider on, we saw dollar signs in our heads. Then, one or both of our horses would peter out toward the end of the race, and we would scream for the rider to do something quick.

Other times, our horse was slow out of the gate and we would yell as if the horse and rider could hear us, "Move faster! Go, go, go!" Then all of a sudden, as if our coaching helped, our horse would slowly sneak up and cross the finish line ahead of the others.

We screamed with joy when this happened. We won money, and the less-favored horse proved himself. Of course, we would brag to our dad that our method of selecting winners was better than his law of averages.

Do you think that just because you take up a seat in your church you have clout with God?

The point is, Christians who sprint quickly coming out of the salvation gate are not always those who win the race. Many don't even finish before fizzling out. Others stick around, but become lazy racers who don't have enough spiritual energy to cross the finish line.

Jesus finished an extremely painful race. He willingly endured mocking, beatings, separation from God, and death on the cross for the salvation of the world. And let us remind you, Jesus died so *you* could live a sin-free, addiction-free life and enjoy the promise of heaven. So why would God be happy to have pew sitters claiming to be Christians? Do you think that just because you take up a seat in your church you have clout with God?

In 1 Corinthians 9:24-27, the Apostle Paul wrote about the Christian race and encouraged followers of Christ to get in shape to finish and win.

"Do you not know that those who run in a race all run, but one receives the prize? Run in such a way that you may obtain it. And everyone who competes for the prize is temperate in all things. Now they do it to obtain a perishable crown, but we for an imperishable crown. Therefore I run thus: not with uncertainty. Thus I fight: not as one who beats the air. But I discipline my body and bring it into subjection, lest, when I have preached to others, I myself should become disqualified."

Everyone has a Job
There are a lot of Christian myths. One is that only certain people are meant to lead and do the work of the ministry. The Bible teaches that everyone has a job to do; that every joint supplies.

In The Solid Rock Road, we don't let participants off the hook because they just can't help who they are. In fact, we believe in getting people on the hook, which is why we don't take this Principle lightly. It seems so simple to teach people to serve God and others, but serving is where most people fail, especially those who are in constant turmoil.

It takes work to be a Christian. When you enter the kingdom of God, you're saying 'yes' to the divine recruiter. You have become a part of a body and joined the Army. Each of these positions requires teamwork, which means you are accountable and responsible to others.

Lazy members of a football team are kicked off the squad. Lazy members of a corporate management team are fired. Lazy Marines are tried for treason. And yet, lazy church members are tolerated and accepted. They have actually become the norm in many Christian circles.

We believe that the only way for you to reach your destiny in God is to live as radical a Christian lifestyle as you did in your sinful nature. Didn't you serve the devil with all your heart? Why do you consistently refuse to serve God and others with the same intensity?

What we believe doesn't really matter. It's what God says that counts, and we have been careful to make sure what we think is in line with Biblical teachings.

Radical is More Normal
When you called on God as a last-ditch effort to get straight, you were most likely living a radical sinful lifestyle. This rendered you financially strapped,

jobless, homeless, and without the support of family. Many of your children were placed in foster care.

With your life in disarray, you began the process of sobriety, which required you to clear your mind, recognize your insanity, take responsibility for your situation, and counteract the collateral damage.

As a new believer, or as a repentant backslider, you were desperate for attention. Many of you needed help mapping out your life's strategy. We're sure good Christian people assisted you along the way and offered personal guidance, rides to church, money, and food, access to work, assistance with court matters, and a million other things you needed and they were willing to give.

This kind of love and support is Biblical and you should receive it graciously. But taken too far, support can turn into co-dependency and those who are trying to do God's will often enter into unhealthy, unbiblical relationships with addicts like you.

Our pastor refers to this type of co-dependent behavior as "ungodly compassion." It feeds on everyone's dysfunction.

It's important you know the difference between godly and ungodly compassion. One is service-oriented and the other is self-seeking. We discussed this in a previous chapter when we noted that co-dependency is a sin and a cycle in which the giver is trying to get something from their service. But this self-seeking aspect of a relationship is most intriguing because the ones who act as rescuers are oftentimes as spiritually unwell as those being rescued.

When we observe this phenomenon, we ask the rescuer, "What are you getting out of this?" Their answers usually fall into one of three categories, with the general responses being, "I want to show them unconditional love," or "If I don't do it, who will?" or "I feel sorry for them." Our favorite is "It's my ministry."

That's when we give them the truth—their co-dependency can be the death of the addict. Sometimes it's good for an addict to realize they have no earthly help in order to understand that God is their only source of hope or help.

In many cases, the right thing for a rescuer to do is get out of the way and let God be God.

Becoming a Servant

Christianity isn't about getting what you can get from God and others; it's about getting liberated from sin so you can live a decent life and model freedom to others.

Over the years, we have identified three types of recovered addicts:

1. **Perpetual takers** — This group expects to be served and will ask more of people than they can possibly give. They usually get what they can from one person, then move on to the next person and take from them.
2. **Modified takers** — This group of people gets the help they need and give a little back here and there.
3. **Grateful takers** — This type of recovered addict is one who appreciates the help, doesn't ask too much for too long, and quickly begins to give back.

Gratitude is vital to your Christian growth. For some people, being a grateful taker comes natural. For others, it goes against their selfish grain. If that's you, it's time to change. No matter how long you stay sober, you can't live a me-centered life because Christianity and selfishness are opposing terms.

 When you practice radical recovery and active Christianity, you become grateful and are gifted with a servant's heart. So evaluate yourself right now and identify the level of selfishness you currently exhibit. While it's true we're all in a continual process of change, there should be evidence you're moving forward.

- Are you obsessed with your own issues?
- In the past week, what have you done to restore or build a relationship with another person?
- When was the last time you thanked someone for supporting you with your recovery?
- Have you recently offered support to someone else?
- How often do you show your friends, spouse or children you love them – through actions, not words?
- List the favors you have asked for this week.
- List the favors you have given this week.
- Have you manipulated anyone to get something you determined you need? If so, how?
- How many times this week have you asked people in your life, "How are you doing?" and actually listened and cared?
- Have you prayed for the needs of others this week?
- In the past three days, how many phone calls have you made to get help for one thing or another?
- In the past three days, how many phone calls have you made offering help to others?
- Do you constantly rescue others at the risk of your own well-being and that of your family members?
- When you agree to rescue someone, are you in the will of God, or are you rescuing out of your own need?
- If you're a chronic rescuer, what need gets met when you're helping someone out of a jam?

Setting a Service Goal

If you're serving God and others, you're in the blessing zone. If you fall short and are struggling to stay clean and sober, don't feel condemned. Instead, see this as an opportunity to turn things around.

Pay attention to your thoughts and actions. Notice how many times you hope to be served versus the number of times you take the initiative to serve others. Then, set a service goal for yourself.

For example, decide to contact two people this week you know who are suffering and pray with them. Make sure you don't cater to their worldly needs, but serve them according` to their need for God. For some, your prayer may be followed up by a simple introduction to Jesus. For other situations, the next step is an invitation to church or a Christian gathering of one sort or the other.

Now for a few words of caution: Do not set yourself up for falling into temptation. We can't tell you the number of times we've seen recovering addicts go to pull people out of the fire only to find themselves burned and in ashes.

Don't underestimate Satan who wants to take you captive again. He waits for you to feel overconfident and to step back into his territory prematurely.

The Holy Spirit comes with spiritual authority, but in the same way new Army recruits are sent to boot camp for training, you have to learn how to fight spiritual battles on behalf of others. As you learned earlier, you have to put on the full armor of God and be trained to wield the sword of the Spirit.

Never allow your acts of service to endanger your spiritual life. If you have a history of relapse, then by all means steer clear of others who are in early recovery or active in their addiction. Instead, serve a single mother by making a meal or offering to babysit. Or serve an elderly couple who would appreciate your coming over to vacuum or repair their home.

Like-Minded Sinners

Separation of like-minded sinners and adherence to same-sin ministry is a man-made method that has the potential to feed into the sin nature of addicts. For some reason, addicts always limit themselves to serving other addicts. But this kind of support isn't promoted in scripture. If it were Biblical, then recovering liars would only serve recovering liars, and recovering gossips would only serve gossips, and recovering worriers would only serve fellow worriers.

Can you imagine a group of recovering gossips meeting several times a week, claiming they are gossips and describing their gossip-centered life one by one? We doubt anyone's secret would be safe in that room!

God pre-determined your ministry, as you learned in the Spiritual Gifts chapter. It is better to discover your true purpose than to cling to your addiction circles. God will use your testimony to bless other addicts along the way, but if you commit to doing God's *perfect* will and not your preconceived concept of what God has planned for your life, you will have a much bigger impact on the world.

If you give yourself fully to serving God how He has planned, then your life will be an amazing adventure. If you don't, you may enjoy some benefits of Christianity, but you limit God in His ability to make your life an amazing legacy.

Paying the Price

If you remain self-centered and allow yourself the luxury of laziness, you may get plenty of rest, but you'll never be satisfied with anything about your life. Not only that, you'll pass the spirit of apathy down to your children and others in your sphere of influence, then wonder why no one in your life is motivated to stay true to their faith.

Your lack of discipline deems you a hypocrite and will send those closest to you down the Yellow Brick Road looking for answers that make more sense to them than Christianity.

Yes, there will be ups and downs. But just like a rollercoaster, you'll have a blast getting roughed up, and in the end, you're glad for the ride.

However, if you want to be used by God in awesome and inspiring ways, and are willing to pay the price in service to God, then get ready for an unbelievable journey!

Yes, there will be ups and downs. But just like a rollercoaster, you'll have a blast getting roughed up, and in the end, you're glad for the ride.

And when your children watch what you do in good times and in bad, they determine in their hearts to stay on the path you've laid out for them.

Jesus as Lord

When you were born again, you proclaimed Jesus as your Lord and Savior. Most of us understand and appreciate the Savior part of this statement, but few like having a Lord over their life. But if Jesus is Lord, He is your master and you are His servant.

We've discussed this in earlier chapters, but it's so important, we're going over it again.

If having God as your master doesn't sit well with you, you're not alone. The very idea that we have a master and are servants of this master goes against our nature. It defies everything we've been taught by society and New Age philosophies that successfully promote independence and the sanctity of self.

Many people recoil at the mention of the word 'Lord'. Some mistake this kind of response as discernment, accepting their long-held belief that

Christianity denies them an identity and forbids them freedom. When their inner voice tells them to escape from the claws of religion, they quickly comply, thereby solidifying their ongoing relationship with the world. You have to admit, it's a great trick Satan uses, and it works much of the time.

> It's not by chance that the word 'Lord' occurs 250 times in the New Testament, making it the most frequently used term to describe Jesus.

Jesus knew that humans would have a negative response to the concept of lordship, so He issued a challenge to his listeners in Luke 6:46: *"Why do you call me, 'Lord, Lord,' and do not do what I say?" (NIV)*

Jesus went on to say that if you hear His words but don't put them into practice, it's like building a house without a foundation: it is so unsteady that the least amount of turbulence will cause it to collapse. In other words, if you don't serve the Master, you're without a Christian foundation and your faith will be destroyed the minute a problem arises.

It's not by chance that the word 'Lord' occurs about 250 times in the New Testament, making it the most frequently used term to describe Jesus. For example, the first words from Saul (who later became the Apostle Paul) at his conversion were, *"Who are you, Lord?"* (Acts 9:5) When doubting Thomas finally came face to face with the resurrected Jesus, his immediate response was, *"My Lord and my God!"* (John 20:28)

The meaning of the word 'Lord' is clear in scripture. The problem is not misunderstanding it; the problem is actually making Jesus Lord of *your* life.

You have a choice, but your refusal to serve the Master means that you choose to serve the devil. You can't have it both ways, even though you want the best of both worlds. For a long time, we couldn't see why everything had to be either black or white when we preferred gray. The middle ground seemed much more fun, safer, freer, and less intimidating. But the middle ground is the most dangerous.

Excuses to Not Serve

There are no limits to the excuses people use to get out of serving God and others. Recently, we spent weeks helping a woman detox from alcohol. For the sake of anonymity, we'll call her Betty.

In Betty's first few days of sobriety, she called one of us every fifteen minutes to report on how she was feeling and to get words of encouragement and prayer. When she'd made it a week without drinking, we celebrated and praised God. By then the phone calls had dwindled to about five per day. By week three, Betty was calling an average of three times a day.

Though we weren't thrilled about the interruption in our life and time, we eagerly answered every call because we had faith that Betty was finally getting it. She had been calling herself a Christian for many years, but was a hardcore alcoholic who enjoyed smoking pot and doing other drugs when they came her way.

It was a great day when Betty stayed sober long enough to attend one of Joy Christian Fellowship's three-day Encounters. We drove her to church on Friday and helped her get settled in. She was in a safe place and in good hands because Jamee was assigned as Betty's guide throughout the process.

Betty shed a lot of tears during the first half of the Encounter and claimed she had finally found her family, after having been rejected by so many other Christians and churches. But during the second half, which helps people understand their role as a Christian, Betty was more like a caged animal. She desperately wanted to leave. Though Betty completed the Encounter, we believe that her self-centered sin nature had declared war against the Christian philosophy of accountability, responsibility, and service—all things that are taught in the last half.

> **Some people prefer chaos to healthy Christianity. They cling to their salvation, but resist the 'Jesus is Lord' concept.**

The day after the Encounter, Betty called and admitted that she had relapsed. We told her to repent and move on. A week or so later, Betty informed us that she couldn't resist the temptation to get drunk. We told her to repent and move on. But when Betty continued to drink then call for prayer and words of encouragement, we quit responding in the same way.

We still cared about Betty, but realized that she only wanted to experience stage one of sobriety and Christianity, which is a lot like stage one in a relationship. It's the fun and exciting part. Everything is new and euphoric. Falling in love brings an emotional high. But the rubber meets the road when the euphoria wears off.

These kinds of cases are not that complex. Some people prefer chaos to healthy Christianity. They cling to their salvation, but resist the 'Jesus is Lord' concept. They come up with a million and one excuses for their lack of commitment and service.

The following are the top six excuses for not serving God and others: (we could write a book on excuses alone.)

Excuse 1: I need to be served right now

New believers are like babies. The Bible says they need milk, not meat, because their spirits aren't mature enough to absorb deep truths. But babies grow up. And while all Christians have to crawl before they walk, at some point everyone must stand on their own two feet.

If you have been a Christian for more than a year, we suggest you remove your bib, get out of the highchair, and start walking out your faith. There are new babies being born all around you. It's time you did some feeding.

You have a job to do, so find out what it is and get to work. Ephesians 4:11,12 says it like this: *"It was he who gave some to be apostles, some to be prophets, some to be evangelists, and some to be pastors and teachers, to prepare God's people for works of service, so that the body of Christ may be built up...." (NIV)*

Excuse 2: I don't want to get too deep into this Christian thing

There's no such thing as getting too deep into Christianity. You're either a disciple or you're not. If you're a disciple, then you're a follower of Jesus, which means you must use the mind of Christ and put spiritual teachings into practice.

If you're only knee-deep in Christianity, you have a problem. First of all, your half-heartedness means you don't care if other people get saved and spiritually fed, as long as you are. And more importantly, your lack of commitment will be judged.

God's view on half-heartedness is unveiled in Revelation 3:15-16, which says, *"I know your works, that you are neither cold nor hot. I could wish you were cold or hot. So then, because you are lukewarm, and neither cold nor hot, I will vomit you out of My mouth."*

Nothing more must be said. We believe the vomiting part of the above scripture makes the point for us.

Excuse 3: I'm not ready

When you took your first drink or did your first drug, you weren't ready for your addiction, but you practiced enough to become an addict. We doubt anyone who serves in a church or a ministry is totally prepared, but for those willing, God gives grace.

When we started The Solid Rock Road, we weren't ready. None of us knew what we were supposed to do. God had provided the Principles, but He didn't offer a detailed how-to manual to put the Principles into action. Instead, we said 'Yes' to the assignment, prayed for insight, and went to our pastor with what we had discovered.

Having our pastor as our covering and the Holy Spirit as our guide, we went to work—ready or not there we were!

So get ready to serve in whatever capacity your church needs. As you serve your church, its members and the world, your personal ministry will unfold.

Excuse 4: I'm too busy

If being busy was a legitimate excuse, then no one would be serving the Master. According to our Day Timers, we have no time to rescue anyone from a fire, let alone facilitate Solid Rock Road groups. Our written schedules are viable from the standpoint that we have families, households, and businesses to run. But we also understand the law of sowing and reaping and know that when we give away our time, we're rewarded with more.

We often get it backwards much. In our minds, it makes sense to take care of our lives and to use our extra time to serve God. But Matthew 6:33 says *"But seek first the kingdom of God and His righteousness, and all these things shall be added to you."*

It makes good spiritual sense to serve God with all your heart. He'll make sure you have time for your life.

Excuse 5: I don't have anything to give

If you've been saved and delivered from your addiction, you have a lot to say about the goodness of God. And, you have a story to tell about Jesus who died on the cross to take away your sins and heal your body. You don't have to be a great speaker or have a theology degree to share the Gospel. You just have to be yourself.

You are unique and have something special to offer people in need. First Peter 4:10 helps us understand the importance of your individuality: *"Each one should use whatever gift he has received to serve others, faithfully administering God's grace in its various forms." (NIV)*

Excuse 6: People want too much from me

We hear this one a lot, especially from those with a taker mentality. If you find it easy to ask a lot from others, but seriously limit the time and resources you give, then you're way outside of the blessing zone. What you must understand is that it's not people that want something from you, it's God. The people in your life are just His messengers.

Malachi 3:18 says, *"And you will again see the distinction between the righteous and the wicked, between those who serve God and those who do not." (NIV)*

This prophet of God is saying that those who don't serve God are wicked, and those who do are righteous.

In Summary

The word 'Christian' is a noun, adjective, and a verb. It's the name for those in the process of becoming Christ-like, and it is a word that represents this action.

Christianity is not like the hammock experience we described in the first few paragraphs of this chapter, although most people wish it was. But if you willingly serve, you will find rest in God, and it will be better than a temporary trip to the Bahamas. In that rest, you will look around and see your children thriving, your joy fulfilled, finances growing, and your relationships getting healthier and happier.

We suggest you savor the sweetness and goodness of God and that you allow the Word of God to guide your life. When you are a true disciple of Christ, otherwise known as a Christian, you will enjoy the fruits of the Spirit, which are love, joy, peace and other blessings described in Galatians 5:22-23.

Afterward:
The Next Best Steps

"Everyone who competes in the games goes into strict training. They do it to get a crown that will not last; but we do it to get a crown that will last forever." (NIV)
— 1 Corinthians 9:25

Congratulations on finishing this book! However, it's not over yet. We expect your journey of discovery along The Solid Rock Road to continue as you process through all the information, put God's Principles into action, and become a model for radical recovery.

There's no doubt we've been single-minded in this book. Our focus has been on recovery and restoration from drugs and alcohol. Our message is that as Christians, we don't have to cope with our addictions, we can be set free.

Nevertheless, the 10 Principles of The Solid Rock Road can be used to overcome any stronghold because they are a template for Christian living. You don't have to be a doper or a drunk to put them to work. You just have to want to change.

Connect with Us
We've bared portions of our soul with you, and in return, we'd like to hear about your breakthroughs, revelations, and victories. Tell us if you've learned something amazing about yourself while reading this book, or how practicing one or more of the 10 Principles has transformed your life.

Send us an email briefly outlining your journey to TheSolidRockRoad@gmail.com. You can also stay in touch, continue to learn, and participate in group discussions by visiting www.thesolidrockroad.com.

We encourage you to share what you have learned with your pastor, friends, and family. Pass the book along to other Christians who struggle with addictions. We believe that The Solid Rock Road recovery ministry leads people to the path of service. We don't promote the program per se. Instead, we promote the transforming power of God.

We believe that the message of radical recovery will spread one person at a time, and from one household to the next, and from one church to another.

We hope to have started a powerful and practical radical recovery revolution!

Links to The Solid Rock Road
We have a presence on the Internet so you can stay connected with us no matter where you live. Here are a few links to get you started. One will lead you to the next.

Website: www.thesolidrockroad.com
Email: TheSolidRockRoad@gmail.com
Twitter: www.twitter.com/solidrockroad
Twitter: www.twitter.com/solidrockroad2

Speaking, Teaching, and Training

Our mission is to share and connect with like-minded individuals, ministry leaders, pastors, and Christian recovery organizations who share our passion for winning the battle for souls, and who agree that God is enough.

We're also taking our message to the streets and making ourselves available to speak, preach, teach, or train. We have a lot to say and believe that God has assigned The Solid Rock Road team to spread the message of freedom from addictions.

To complement this book, we've written *The Solid Rock Road Facilitator's Manual*, which provides instructions on how to facilitate groups. These groups meet weekly for 10 straight weeks, working on each Principle, one at a time.

Thank you for allowing us the privilege of writing what's in our hearts based on our experiences in the world, the Word of God and our Christian recovery ministry.

We will continue praying for your soul. And please pray for ours!

The Holistic Approach to Christianity

Although we've written this book with a focus on freedom from addictions, this is only one piece of the larger Christian living puzzle. We see The Solid Rock Road recovery ministry as one element in a holistic approach to Christianity.

God wants every Christian to live a holy and wholesome life. In the Merriam-Webster's online dictionary, the word 'wholesome' is defined as "Promoting health or well-being in mind and spirit: Sound in body, mind, or morals."

Our lives become models of Christianity. If all we're trying to do is cope or get clean and sober for a while, what are we modeling?

Each one of us is responsible to look at all aspects of our lives and to move into higher-level habits and behaviors. Yes, these are involved processes, but mankind is a work in progress, with the ultimate goal of expressing the glory of God.

"But we all, with unveiled face, beholding as in a mirror the glory of the Lord, are being transformed into the same image from glory to glory, just as by the Spirit of the Lord." (2 Corinthians 3:18)

While The Solid Rock Road is focused on the individual, our ministry is totally devoted to the restoration and sanctity of the family. Our willingness to fight and win the battle of addictions for ourselves and others has resulted in the miraculous.

At the same time, our pastor has challenged us to expect victory in other aspects of our lives, including our marriages, family relationships, finances, careers and parenting. And, while working on character development, we have moved forward with educational endeavors, leadership and discipleship skills, as well as other attributes necessary to build the kingdom of God and leave a legacy for generations to come.

Sharing Resources

We attend Joy Christian Fellowship in Medford, Oregon, which was started in 1983 by Pastors Steve and Kim Schmelzer. We've learned what it means to be part of the Army of God at Joy because the leadership has embraced the holistic approach to Christianity and is engaged in the spiritual battle for souls.

We practice what we preach because of the message we've heard, and we have a heart to share it because it's part of our church's DNA.

Our pastors are connected and accessible for the purpose of promoting the work of the local church, spreading the Gospel around the world, and to emphasize the Word of God and the standards given in the Bible.

Joy is not the only church with a pastor who preaches purity, trains and educates his congregation, and presents a holistic approach to Christianity from the pulpit. However, it is a church willing to share resources and connect with other church pastors and leaders who are holiness oriented.

If you're interested in connecting and learning more about Joy's proven method for training and educating its members (including access to Zoe Bible College online), visit www.joychristianfellowship.com.

Our Mission

When we set The Solid Rock Road recovery ministry in motion, we believed we were answering a call from God. In a meeting we held to further develop our vision, our director, Jerry Pineda, made the statement, "This isn't The Yellow Brick Road. This is The Solid Rock Road, the path of righteousness in God.

That's how we ended up with the name of our ministry. From that day forward, we all understood the mission. We were given a path and our job was to teach others how to Follow the Solid Rock Road.

A Final Message from Jerry Pineda, Director of The Solid Rock Road

"This book has just about said it all, but my personal message to those of you who want freedom from addictions is this: Don't be afraid to suffer. Be more afraid not to. You're not alone or without a purpose when you're suffering for Christ. Most importantly, make sure to suffer all the way to the cross as Jesus did for you. It's time to finish what you started. Your new life begins when you die to yourself and are resurrected into the life and love of the Lord Jesus Christ."

Made in the USA
Charleston, SC
21 March 2010